TRANSFORMING
Renewal Against the Odds
1981-1994

TRANSFORMING ROVER

Renewal Against the Odds
1981-1994

ALAN PILKINGTON

Bristol
Academic
Press

Published by
Bristol Academic Press
7 Grange Park
Westbury-on-Trym
Bristol
BS9 4BU

Copyright © Alan Pilkington and Bristol Academic Press, 1996

All rights reserved. No part of this publication may be reproduced, stored in a retrieval system, or transmitted, in any form or by any means, electronic, mechanical, photocopying, recoding, or otherwise, without the prior permission of Bristol Academic Press.

British Library Cataloguing-in-Publication Data.
A catalogue record for this book is
available from the British Library.

ISBN 0 9513762 3 3

Printed in Great Britain by
Antony Rowe Ltd.
Chippenham
England
SN14 6QA.

Contents

Preface ix

1 Striving for Organisational Renewal 1

2 The Manufacturing Revolution 24

3 Collaboration or Collapse? 58

4 Keeping the Options Open: Warwick University 90

5 An Impossible Leap? 115

6 Examples of Success 131

7 Innovation Roadblock or Gateway? 148

8 Restructuring the European Car Industry: Lessons from Rover 163

Index 173

List of Tables, Figures and Plates

Tables

1.1	International Comparison of Car Production, 1950-90	2
1.2	Capital Injections into British Leyland, 1975-84	13
1.3	British Leyland's Non-Commercial Vehicle Ranges, 1978 and 1981	14
1.4	British Leyland's Models and Production Output, 1970 to 1994	15
1.5	Rover Group Share of UK Car Registrations	20
1.6	Profit and Loss at Rover, 1981-94	21
2.1	World Auto Production in 1990 by Manufacturer (Ranked by Volume of Car Production)	26
2.2	IMVP Summary of Assembly Plant Characteristics	28
2.3	Abernathy's Chronicle of Innovations in the Auto Industry	36
2.4	Comparisons of Product Development in Japan and the West	41
2.5	The Four Phase Model of Supplier Relationships	52
2.6	Suppliers to Major Car Manufacturers, 1988	54
3.1	Significant Relationships in the International Auto Industry	60
3.2	A Taxonomy of Inter-Firm Arrangements	63
3.3	The Shared Experiences of Rover's Board of Directors: 1994	66
3.4	Honda Car Production, 1963-92	68
3.5	Sakiya's Periodisation of Honda Motor's History	70
3.6	Comparison of Rover and Honda at the Start of the Relationship	74
3.7	Rover Car Production Split by Platform	80
3.8	Productivity Development in BL-Rover, 1955-94	85

TABLES, FIGURES AND PLATES vii

4.1	Changes in Rover's Stock Turnover Rates, 1955-94	106
4.2	The Work of Rover's ATC Groups, 1992	108
5.1	Existing Literature Concerning Organisational Renewal	116
5.2	The Adoption of Breakthrough at Rover	121
5.3	Pre-Privatisation Highlights, 1991	127
6.1	Comparison of K-Series Engine	132
7.1	Freeman's Ten Characteristics of Successful Innovating Firms	150
7.2	Innovations Studied in the Rover Group in 1992	152
7.3	Summary of Study into Innovation in the Rover Group	154
8.1	Cars in Use (Not New Sales) and Levels of Ownership in Europe, 1967-91	165
8.2	The Cycles of European Car Sales, 1973-91	166
8.3	Crude Cars per Employee per Year for Various Countries, 1979-89	167

Figures

1.1	Pralahad and Hamel's Model of the Core Competencies of the Corporation	5
1.2	History of the Rover Organisation	11
2.1	Automotive Assembly Plant Production Process	29
2.2	The Effect of Simultaneous Engineering on Product Development	42
2.3	The Structure of the Japanese Auto Supply Network	51
4.1	The Development of the Relationship between Rover and Warwick University	103

Plates

1.1	Morris Assembly Line, Cowley, 1933	16
2.1	The Austin Body Production Line, Longbridge, 1926-27	30
2.2	The Mini Body-in-White Line of the 1970s, Longbridge	31

2.3	Robot Welding of the R8, Longbridge, 1990s	32
2.4	Automated Paint Spraying, Longbridge, 1990s	33
2.5	The Robotic Glazing Cell in R8 Final Assembly, Longbridge, 1990s	38
3.1	Honda and Rover Engineers with a Longbridge-Assembled Honda Concerto, 1990s	77
6.1	The A-Series Production Line, Longbridge, 1990s	134
6.2	The Longbridge K-Series Assembly Line, 1990s	137
8.1	John Towers and Bernd Pischetsrieder with an MGRV8 at Gaydon, 1994	169

Preface

Transforming Rover: Renewal Against the Odds, 1981-1994, explains how Rover turned itself around from the brink of disaster to become an example of manufacturing best practice for the 1990s and the target for the surprise takeover by BMW — a takeover that saw the end of an indigenous British motor industry. Few UK companies have been able to match the levels of manufacturing performance coming from Japan. Rover has achieved this by opportunistically exploiting ideas from many places and implanting them into the operating and intellectual core of the company. The sources of the renewal include Honda, academia, management consultants and suppliers. Rover, using this strategy, has produced many highly acclaimed cars and become a shining example of modern industrial practice. The revolution, however, did not lead to the financial recovery of the firm. This book plots the successes, failures and lessons of the Rover revolution and its impact on the workings of this large, complex manufacturing company. The Rover story also has wider implications for the future of the automotive industry, with many of the forces which beset Rover emerging in the European market.

The transformation of Rover is explored in three sections. The first deals with the nature of organisational transformation, manufacturing innovation and the management of capabilities. The heart of the text is concerned with the actual renewal of manufacturing at Rover, and the tribulations and problems it experienced. Chapter 1 sets out the reasons why renewal became necessary, and considers current theories which seek to explain organisational transformation. It also includes an account of some of the key events in the history of Rover, there being many resonances in the story before 1981 which reappear in the manufacturing-led renewal of the modern company. The second chapter concentrates on the emergence of new manufacturing approaches which have been powerful forces for change in the car industry. The decline of the British motor industry, and the rise, first, of American firms, and then Japanese, is related to changing markets and new methods of assembly and management, and not to design or marketing techniques.

The second section addresses the origins of Rover's transformation. The company generated its renewal using several sources of capability input. Some of the ideas took root, whilst others were knee-jerk reactions to pressures from within the organisation. Chapter 3 is an account of Rover's involvement with Honda, the early success which Honda's expertise brought, and the turmoil that followed. It also considers strategies resulting from the unstable nature of the joint venture with Honda, strategies intended to keep open other sources of capability. The process of renewal was not smooth, since there were several factions in the firm which at times adopted differing and conflicting strategies. Rover's factions enlisted the help of different manufacturing engineering experts, academics and management consultants. Chapter 4 is concerned with the formation of the much discussed partnership with Warwick University, which developed as manufacturing managers within the organisation tried to keep an escape route from Honda open. However, the story of the Rover Group is not just one of tactical incrementalism; the company did take significant leaps in the dark. A particular example which illustrates the way in which Rover management threw caution to the wind is discussed in Chapter 5 — the enlistment of external consultants.

The third section considers how far these attempts at change have proved successful, and weighs the evidence for the claimed turnaround of a firm which has lost control of its future, has failed to increase sales beyond the levels of ten years ago, and has failed to produce a consistent profit. Chapter 6 deals with examples of success at Rover including the K-series engine and the introduction of Japanese working practices. These, however, are negated to some extent by the disturbing fact that, though Rover may have recovered, it never managed to restore its fortunes to a level which might concern its competitors. During the Honda years, Rover's output declined and the profitability of the firm was not sufficient to win the prize of an independent and prosperous future. Rover failed to take full advantage of what it had access to, and this ultimately led to its sale to BMW. Chapter 7 builds on the preceding chapter to look at innovation processes in the Rover group as a whole, drawing examples from Land Rover and the car manufacturing parts of the business. It discusses processes of innovation in each section of the firm, and how these different approaches, which have produced different results, are influenced by the markets within which the firm has to navigate. At Land Rover, the pace of change has been much slower, yet innovations generated within the firm do take root. In car manufacturing, however, changes have been introduced from outside, sometimes generating resentment on the part of the managers and workers who have to live with them. As a result the innovations are not completely accepted and can become difficult to maintain within the organisation.

The final chapter raises a number of themes which pertain more generally to the European motor industry. Three features of the Rover story are becoming apparent in the more general conditions faced by European manufacturers. First, the Rover case illustrates how changing market fortunes undermined the financial performance of the business; lessons can be drawn from this for the future European car market. Secondly, the Rover case shows that at each stage purposive plans and policies designed to reduce costs and improve resource efficiency came to nought because they failed to transform the financial operating characteristics of the business. Again, broader lessons can be learnt for the European cars business. Finally, now that the relationship with Honda has ended and BMW has claimed what was left of a hollowed out business, the case of Rover provides an example of a path already being followed by weak European companies which become dependent on others for product and process innovation. In the end, weak companies are often taken over and restructured.

My thanks go to Charles Harvey, Bob Fitzgerald, Colin Haslam and all my colleagues at Royal Holloway, University of London, for their personal and intellectual support. Encouragement was given throughout by Peter Clark of the University of Aston in Birmingham, who supervised my doctoral studies on which this book is based. My fiancée Bernadette deserves special thanks for her patience in putting up with the long hours I spent at the word processor and for keeping me sane at home. Martin Will, technical editor of Bristol Academic Press, offered many helpful suggestions. I have been fortunate to be able to include photographs depicting some of the changes at Rover. These come from the Rover Group and the British Motor Industry Heritage Trust. Both institutions were very helpful in dealing with my requests. I would also like to thank Mr Ian Strachan, Director of Corporate Communications at Rover, for his help and especially for thoroughly checking the manuscript.

Finally, I would like to say that the British car industry has been a fascinating subject for study. I hope that, even though the days of mass-produced British cars have passed, the industry will continue to provide the jobs and economic value so deeply needed in the UK.

Alan Pilkington
School of Management
Royal Holloway, University of London
November 1995

Picture Credits

Cover: The R8 Laser Body Measuring Station at Longbridge.

Cover, Plates 2.3, 2.4, 2.5, 3.1, 6.1, 6.2, 8.1 © Rover Group.
Plates 1.1, 2.1, 2.2 © British Motor Industry Heritage Trust.

1

Striving for Organisational Renewal

> *Only if the company is conceived as a hierarchy of core competencies, core products, and market-focused business units will it be fit to fight.*[1]

Few companies have been able to match the rapid rise of the Japanese car manufacturers, a rise which is founded on manufacturing innovation and efficiency. The description of these innovations and their impact on performance created a stir when the five-year $5 million International Motor Vehicle Programme (IMVP) released *The Machine that Changed the World* in 1990 and introduced the phrase 'lean production'[2] to the vocabulary of management. The message from the IMVP was clear: Japanese manufacturing techniques were so far in advance of anything the North Americans, or the even worse Europeans, have to offer, that the rest of the world had better take note or be faced with a very uncertain future.

One Western company that is generally perceived to have made a transformation that matches the Japanese is Rover, once apparently doomed. The sale of Rover to BMW in 1994 marked the end of a nine-year period of restructuring and realignment in the company, during which Rover's manufacturing capabilities were renewed. Rover's approach has been to take ideas from many places and absorb them into the company. The causes of the remarkable renewal include collaboration with Honda, together with other projects involving the academic world, management consultants, manufacturers of equipment and suppliers of parts. The theme which runs throughout the transformation is one of continual change and upheaval in the organisation.

The car industry, being one of the biggest and most influential in the global economy, has been the source of many revolutionary changes in operational strategy, and faces radical upsets every decade. No other mature industrial sector has been so totally transformed since 1940. The market, early on, was largely the province of national players in the United States and Europe; next came a period of remarkable growth dominated by the US giants until the 1980s, when the Japanese moved to the top of the league table (see Table 1.1).[3] Today, the trend of constant change in car manufacture continues, with the emergence of transnational corporations with overseas manufacturing plants, and is being further affected by the arrival of new competition from the Far East. The transition is further fuelled by the re-emergence of a few European companies which once seemed certain to be lost.

Table 1.1
International Comparison of Car Production, 1950-90

Year	Japan	USA	UK	Germany	France	Italy	Canada
1950	1,594	6,665,863	522,515	219,409	257,292	101,310	284,076
1955	20,268	7,920,186	897,560	762,205	561,465	230,978	375,028
1960	165,094	6,674,796	1,352,728	1,816,779	1,175,301	595,907	325,752
1965	969,176	9,305,561	1,722,045	2,733,732	1,423,365	1,103,932	710,711
1970	3,178,708	6,550,203	1,640,966	3,527,864	2,458,038	1,719,715	940,389
1975	4,568,120	6,717,177	1,267,695	2,907,819	2,546,154	1,348,544	1,044,822
1980	7,038,108	6,375,506	923,744	3,520,934	2,938,581	1,445,221	846,777
1985	7,646,816	8,184,821	1,047,973	4,166,686	2,632,366	1,389,156	1,077,935
1990	9,947,972	6,077,449	1,295,611	4,660,657	3,294,815	1,874,672	1,076,119

Source: Society of Motor Manufacturers and Traders (SMMT), *Motor Industry of Great Britain, 1993: World Automotive Statistics* (London, 1993), p. 54.

Porter's work on what makes successful organisations[4] has become established as a solid starting-point for understanding competitive advantage. In his earlier work, *Competitive Strategy*, Porter examined the micro aspects of industrial success: the strategies of successful organisations and the approaches which work best. More recently, in *The Competitive Advantage of Nations*, he has observed that particular industries seem almost predetermined to flourish or fail in certain countries, in response to particular commercial environments. An example of this, some would consider, was the nationalisation of British Leyland (BL). It was widely claimed at the time that the financial crutch provided by government would eventually cause the firm to atrophy; that is to say, that government-provided security would drain the company of what was left of its competitive spirit, so that it would never be able to survive unaided, and would simply remain a huge burden on the Treasury. In short, the British economy was no longer friendly to car manufacture. The opposite view is that government intervention provided a much needed period of security, without which the ramshackle organisation would have been sunk without trace by far more efficient competitors.

Similarly, Chandler's historical explorations of corporate America[5] have been the starting point of many forays into further understanding success in commercial organisations. By examining in detail the development of organisational structures, Chandler and many followers have been able to identify, study and explain patterns of organisational change. What is particularly striking is his demonstration of just how often radical change in organisations is a necessary condition of success. Successful firms will be constantly changing their methods in response to a changing environment. Quinn, in *Strategies for Change: Logical Incrementalism*,[6] has confirmed this finding, in its opposite form: firms which conservatively stick to old working practices and management strategies are very likely to become uncompetitive. Miller and Friesen, in *Organisations: A Quantum View*,[7] took this idea further by analysing the transition of organisations in the light of the typological configurations proposed by Mintzberg in *Structure in Fives*.[8]

Mintzberg found patterns whereby the nature of the organisational structure was reflected in the way that transition between typologies took place. He derived them from the tensions created by the influence of different groups in the organisations. For example, the pull of the technological staff away from the thinking of the strategists shifts the balance of power from the simple bureaucracy to what Mintzberg termed the machine bureaucracy, where standardisation takes precedence over direct supervision. Similarly, new power structures arise from the increased influence of the operating core in either professionalising skills in the bureaucracy, or co-operating together in what Mintzberg termed the adhocracy. A conglomerate, or divisionalised, form of organisation results when the middle-line managers pull towards standardising the outputs of all departments in the firm.

Miller and Friesen showed that unsuccessful conservative firms would eventually be so greatly out of touch with the market that when they finally recognised the need for changes, these had to be far greater than would ever have been required as part of a continuing process. The history of Rover, an account of which forms the latter part of this chapter, is an example of this. Besides describing organisational typologies used to explain transformations in firms, Mintzberg has also helped to develop a longitudinal-historical approach to studying strategy and organisational change. By examining the historical performance of individual firms, Mintzberg's method allows key strategies to be traced back to key decisions. His method was used throughout this study of Rover to elucidate the significant strategies which led to much of the manufacturing renewal, alongside the many and complicated unrealised strategies present in the Rover organisation.

Recent literature has arrived at a deeper insight into organisational success and the forces within organisations which act to produce transformations. This insight has been achieved by identifying the particular skills and capabilities possessed by individual organisations. The method, as originally discussed by Prahalad and Hamel,[9] was primarily developed as a means of explaining the reasons for the repeated success of some firms. Some organisations have acquired strengths in certain technologies which give them an in-built competitive advantage. The capabilities of some organisations are very difficult to identify and even harder for competitors to copy or acquire. Prahalad and Hamel termed these 'core competencies' (see Figure 1.1).

Figure 1.1
Pralahad and Hamel's Model of the Core Competencies of the Corporation

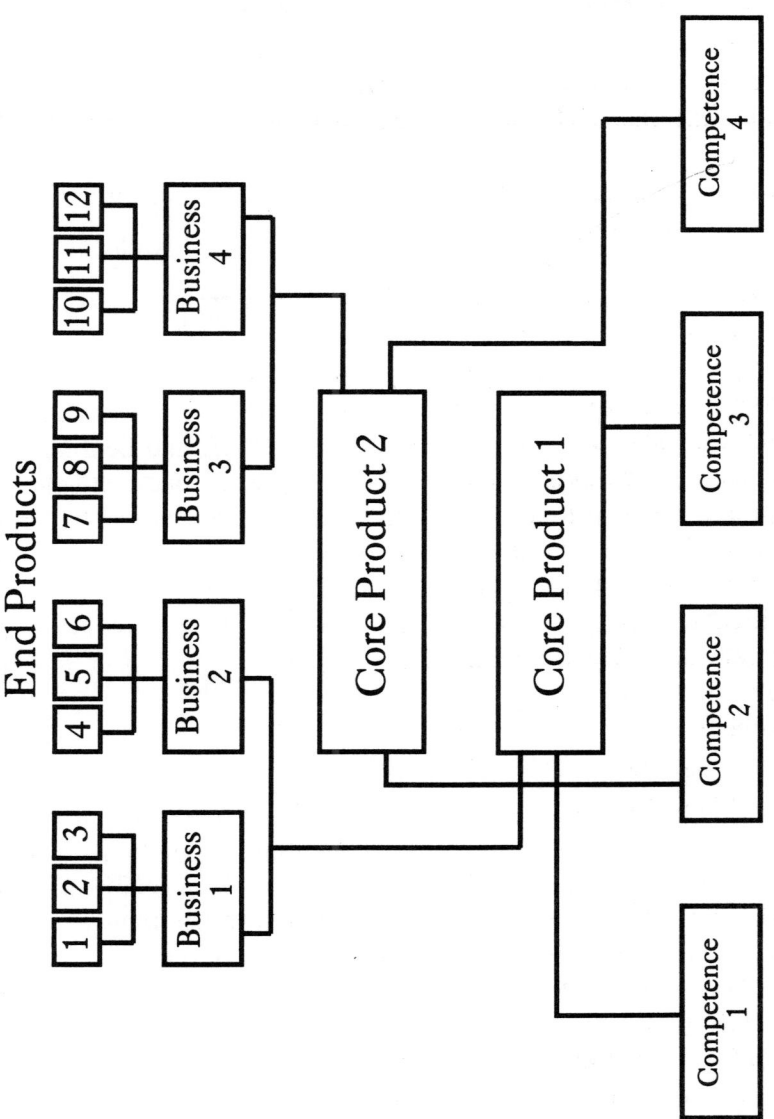

C.K. Pralahad and G. Hamel, 'The Core Competence of the Corporation', *Harvard Business Review* (May-June 1990), p. 81.

Kay extends the definition of competencies to include the continuity and stability of a 'distinctive structure of relationships with employees, customers, and suppliers'.[10] Kay argues that capability alone is not sufficient to guarantee success, and that firms must also be aware of the markets in which they operate through an effective corporate strategy, whether arrived at deliberately or accidentally. This competency-based perspective is used to explain the manufacturing renewal at Rover, the individual capabilities being identified using Mintzberg's method[11] of tracking the historical development of strategies back to key decisions. Plotting the strategies which led to the firm's acquisition or loss of certain capabilities produces a model of how the manufacturing renewal occurred.

What has emerged from several case histories is a familiar sequence, in which initial success is followed by complacency, laziness, and failure, which in turn leads to radical reorganisation and the acquisition of new capabilities, followed by renewal. Here is a key business development process for the 1990s and beyond which is to be found in the story of Rover's manufacturing renewal: the company was the sum of formerly successful parts which failed to react to changes in the market and operating conditions in their industry, and which subsequently nearly disappeared. However, the danger provided a stimulus for the firm to fight to acquire the skills and knowledge which enabled it to re-establish a competitive platform in the industry. In many examples of rejuvenated organisations we may observe a coherent strategy which underwrites the renewal process. This is true of Rover only up to a point. It is true that in successive eras the company has developed coherent business plans, the latest of which is the QS2000. In contrast to the assertions of management, however, we find that the many different parts of the organisation often acted secretly, or in competition with other parts of the firm. This failure to build a totally cohesive organisation is a feature of firms which have recurrent financial problems and are driven by short-term considerations. At the end of the day, it is hard to justify the claim so often made by Rover executives that at the heart of the corporate rejuvenation, the company's managers were wedded to a single unifying strategy.[12]

Until the takeover by BMW, Rover was the only survivor of the once great British motor industry. Although it was the amalgamation of many British car manufacturers (see Figure 1.2), the character of both the Rover that entered into the relationship with Honda and the present Rover company was largely shaped by a threefold ancestry. First, the original Rover company whose strategies and market stance were assimilated by the board of directors under Graham Day; second, the Austin company, whose Longbridge manufacturing plant remains the production volume cornerstone of the firm; and third, a combination of the Morris and Pressed Steel firms, created under the BL regime at the Cowley works in Oxford.

The Rover company started in 1877 when two Coventry men, John Kemp Starley and William Sutton, formed a partnership to produce pennyfarthing cycles and tricycles.[13] Starley was from a family with a history in cycle manufacture and development. His uncle was James Starley, who was referred to as 'the father of the cycle industry' and was commemorated by a monument on the Green in Coventry. Starley and Sutton first used the name of Rover in 1884 on one of their tricycles. Starley, despite his extensive work on tricycles, believed that the future development of the machines lay not with cumbersome three-wheelers or dangerous penny-farthing bicycles, and set out to develop a machine which would be as safe as a three-wheeler but as light as a penny-farthing. The result was the 1885 Rover Safety Bicycle which, after a slow start, redefined the bicycle. The Rover became the pattern which all cycles followed for about 100 years, until the introduction of modern materials in the 1980s.[14] The Rover Safety Cycle also provided the impetus for the establishment of a large UK cycle industry which in turn laid the foundations of the UK car industry. At the height of the boom in 1896, Starley issued shares in the firm. The Rover Cycle Company was formed and became increasingly successful.

Its first venture into motor transport followed in 1902 with the Imperial Rover Motor Cycle, a two-and-a-quarter horse-power machine selling for £55. This was followed in 1911 by a highly successful three-and-a-half horse-power machine which won many touring prizes. The company's first car, an eight horse-power model designed by Edmond Lewis, was produced in 1904. In 1906 the company introduced new capital and became the Rover Company Ltd. Rover developed several models before the outbreak of the First World War, including 6 and 12 h.p. vehicles and a 20 h.p. tourer which won the 1907 International Tourist Trophy race in the Isle of Man. During the war, Rover produced cycles, motor cycles and also munitions, tank gears and Sunbeam cars with ambulance- and staff-car bodies, and Maudslay three-ton lorries for government contracts.

After the war, the company introduced the famous 8 h.p. air-cooled car produced at its new factory in Tyseley, Birmingham. More than 17,000 vehicles were sold between 1920 and 1925. The success of its cars encouraged the company to leave the motor cycle business in 1923. The economic troubles of the early 1930s led Rover to reorganise its activities and introduce S.B. Wilks as managing director. Wilks' strategy was to produce a limited number of vehicles with the highest possible standard of comfort, refinement and performance. The vehicles were made by hand and relied heavily on using wood fascias and leather to promote a sturdy, reliable and luxurious feel. The company promoted the crafted nature of its products and reflected this in its production facilities, which were specifically designed to aid the craftsmen in producing quality vehicles. The success of the craft approach was interrupted by the Second World War, when the company turned its hand to making aero engines, aircraft wings and vehicle bodies. During this time, the firm's engineering and design personnel were involved in developing the Whittle jet propulsion gas turbines which were eventually manufactured by Rolls Royce, a capability Rover was to use again in the 1950s and 1960s. Whipp and Clark[15] argue that this retention of craft-based techniques and work organisation was at the heart of the company's success after the Second World War, but led to disastrous problems in managing the eventual transition to modern mass production methods during the 1970s.

At the end of the war, steel was in short supply and allocations could only be acquired if products could generate export sales. The company's answer to this problem was the corrosion-resistant aluminium-bodied Land Rover, which has been remarkably successful, selling over a million vehicles in over 180 different countries. The Land Rover's sales were given an extra boost when the government decided that because the product was made of aluminium and was originally conceived as an agricultural vehicle, it was exempt from purchase tax. The original Land Rover has been transformed over the years into a whole family of products, including the Range Rover, which was developed in the 1970s. Where it had once been alone in the sector, it began to face competition from vehicles like the Nissan Patrol and Mercedes G-Wagon. Land Rover therefore extended the Land Rover design into the Defender and Discovery in the 1980s and introduced a redesigned Range Rover in 1994. After the war the Rover company continued to develop its quality cars, including the P series of Rover 60, 80, 90, 100, 105, 110, 3.5 litre Coupe models and the 1963 Car of the Year, the Rover 2000. The company also used its expertise in gas turbines to develop the JET 1, the world's first gas turbine propelled car, in 1950. Several gas-turbined prototypes followed, including two which took part in the 1963 and 1965 Le Mans 24-hour races.

The company remained one of the most profitable British car manufacturers right through the 1965 merger with Alvis, which was prompted by the need to cut costs by combining production volumes. The new company developed the 2000TC (twin carburetter) and 2000 Automatic which won the Automobile Association's Gold Medal for its safety features. Rover became a wholly-owned subsidiary of the Leyland Motor Corporation Ltd in 1966 at a time of great concentration in the UK car industry. In the same year, it launched the 3500 (with a similar body style to the 2000). This was the last Rover car in the true Wilks tradition. Leyland took over the British Motor Corporation (BMC) in 1968. The new BLMC organisation was a massive concern, encompassing almost all the UK motor manufacturers, the pedigree of which is summarised in Figure 1.2. The experiences of the firms which formed the new BLMC were all very similar to those of Rover: they were small family concerns which entered the motor age from other sectors of the transport market. Later they adopted mass production manufacturing, before amalgamating in order to remain competitive.

The legacy of Leyland within the modern Rover enterprise stems from the mass production based Austin company, which provided the bulk of Leyland's sales. It still exists in the form of the Longbridge assembly plant in Birmingham, which nowadays produces the bulk of Rover products. The Austin Motor Company was the fulfilment of Herbert Austin's dream 'to motorise the common man'.[16] Austin started in motor manufacturing after taking charge of a Wolseley factory in Birmingham that built sheep shearing equipment for the Australian market. The firm's prospects were hit by a string of faulty machines and needed to broaden its base away from the damaged market. They moved into machine tools and bicycles, and in 1895 Austin produced Britain's first motor car. Wolseley and Austin parted company soon after, leaving Austin to start his own firm, producing motor cars with the financial backing of Frank Kayser, one of Wolseley's steel suppliers. Kayser had been personally impressed with Austin. The success of the cars and the development of the firm is detailed in Church's biography of Austin, but the essence was that Austin was an innovator who introduced engineering excellence into all his activities, including production lines, to make cheap small cars, targeted at ordinary people, rather than the wealthy customers sought by Rover. The influence of Austin on the modern Rover can be seen at the Longbridge works, where the Plant Director still sits in a wood panelled office with a portrait of Austin on the wall.

Austin's great rival, William Morris (later Lord Nuffield), started in the motor industry by selling cars, which helped him formulate his ideas as to what the motorist was looking for. He was also influenced by the arrival of the Model T and developed his own response, the Morris Oxford.[17] Morris went to Detroit to see how the Americans managed to produce cars so cheaply, at the same time placing large orders for the cheaper parts used in his own vehicles.[18] The success of Morris Motors matched that of Austin as they battled to see who could capture the custom of the ordinary motorist. Morris's use of external suppliers to keep his piece costs down, and to minimise the investment needed to develop new models, can be seen in today's Rover. The present Rover Cowley works is on the site of Morris's body supplier, Pressed Steel. Cars were first produced there during the reorganisation of the Ryder era.

Financial problems beset the BLMC organisation in a succession of crises from the autumn of 1973.[19] The company was losing money on most of its models, which were beginning to show their age in a stagnating market. The company had overstretched itself in the attempt to become large enough to do battle with powerful new competitors based in Europe and Japan and with the increasingly competitive Ford UK and Vauxhall. These events were compounded by the oil crisis, the three-day week, and deteriorating economic prospects in the UK due to a rapid increase in inflation. Constraints introduced by the management in order to stem the flow of money from the company caused widespread and notorious industrial unrest in the firm's many plants. These problems caused pre-tax profits to fall from £68m in 1973 to losses of £16m for the first half of 1974.[20]

Figure 1.2
History of the Rover Organisation

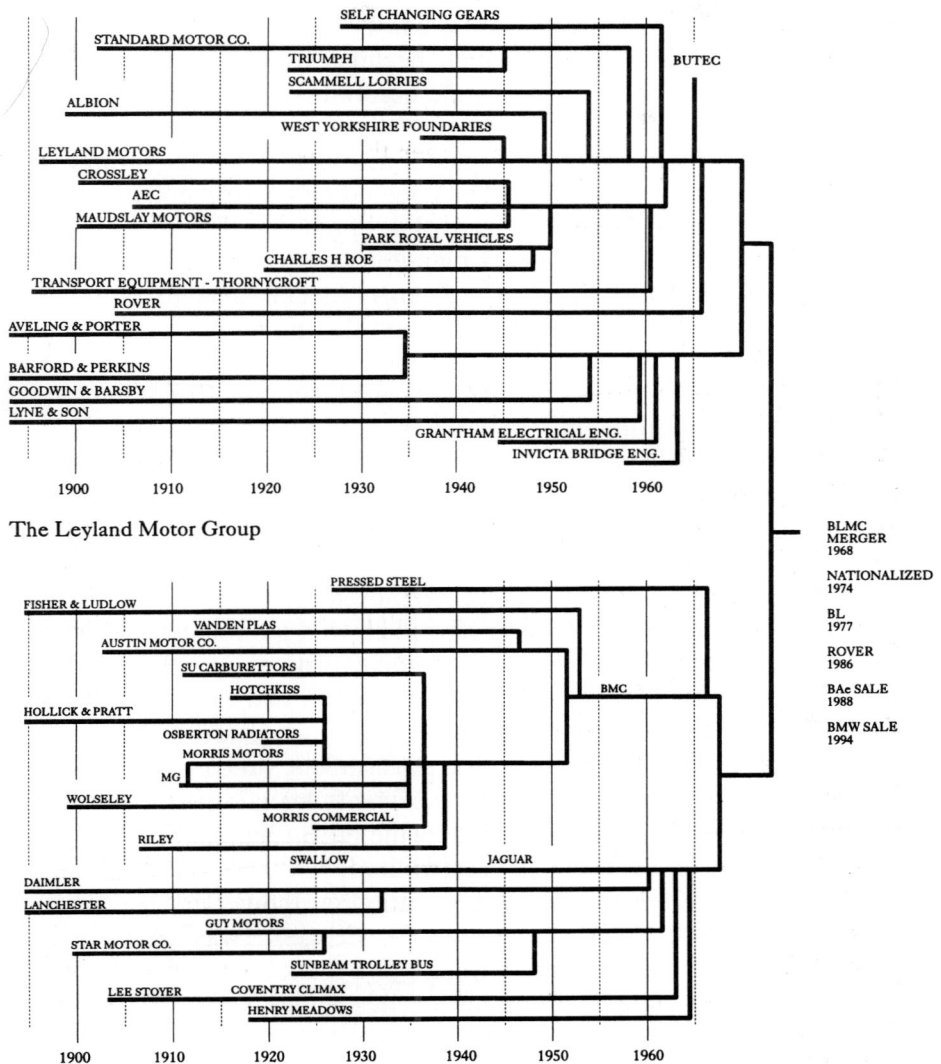

Source: P. Shuttleworth, 'Rover: An Essay on Company History, Current Organisation and Personnel and Industrial Relations' (Unpublished M.Sc. thesis, Lanchester Polytechnic, Coventry, 1977), Appendix 1.

The company could no longer support itself, let alone fund its expansion-based recovery plans. The government was formally invited to intervene in December 1974. The first result of passing control to the government was a Parliamentary Study, 'British Leyland: The Next Decade', which became widely known as the Ryder Plan, after the chairman of the committee responsible for the report.

The Ryder Plan established guidelines which the government required the company to follow. The concluding recommendations of the report were that 'British Leyland should not diversify away from the industry and should remain a manufacturer in all sectors',[21] and it gave support to BLMC's original expansion plans. The government supported the Ryder Plan on the condition that there was a 'substantial programme of product rationalisation',[22] and in the hope that greater exports would generate extra cost reductions. The company developed a mass production range of Rover cars, code-named SD1, using the original Rover works and employees. The transition from the craft-based production methods with which the firm was familiar and the use of unproved or underdeveloped technology were arguably too much for it to cope with. The SD1 range was one of the failures which characterised the nationalised BL organisation.

The Ryder policy was at first pursued slowly, but the appointment of Michael Edwardes as Chief Executive Officer in 1977 added impetus to the transformation. The corporation had not really been slimmed down since the Ryder report's recommendations were made public, and had become a soak for government funds. The capital injections are summarised in Table 1.2. The financial involvement of the British Government was handled by the NEB (National Enterprise Board), a body newly established from the IRC (Industrial Relations Corporation) to generate finance for struggling industries.[23]

The first task which Edwardes undertook was the rapid rationalisation of the company's model and market structures, along the lines of the original proposals of the Ryder Plan. This is an example of a recurrent feature of Rover — the existence of dormant strategies which have been neither shelved nor implemented. The Ryder Plan's rationalisation aspects remained in the organisation waiting to be enacted despite the delay. When Edwardes joined the company, BL had singularly failed to take note of the simplest requirement of amalgamation, and remained a many-branched, sprawling organisation, various sections of which competed with others. The names Rover, Triumph and Austin were different, but many of the products were aimed at the same markets. Furthermore (or possibly in consequence), the company was producing far more vehicles than it could ever hope to sell, and in this was beginning to resemble some of those huge, pointless (from an economic point of view) ventures of Soviet Communism. Edwardes was quick to get to work. This period of model reduction is shown in Table 1.3 and Table 1.4. Edwardes himself referred to the phase as 'The Term of Shrinking';[24] it led to the ending of production at Speke and Solihull, and at Seneffe in Belgium. The model rationalisation nearly halved production capacity from 687,875 units in 1977 to 395,820 in 1980 (see Table 1.4). Offsetting this reduction was the creation of what is now Rover's Large Car Business Unit, the Cowley plant. At Cowley, the Pressed Steel body-making plant was re-designed to produce shells for BL's new model range. This plant had once served the Morris assembly line at Cowley in the 1930s.

Table 1.2
Capital Injections into British Leyland, 1975-84

Year	Capital Injections Into British Leyland (£)
1975-76	£46m — share issue, £200m — nationalisation
1976-77	£70m — NEB, £30m — Government, Industry Act
1977-78	£50m — NEB
1978-79	£300m — NEB, £150m — Government, Industry Act
1979-80	£175m — NEB
1980-81	£300m — NEB
1981-82	£620m — NEB
1982-83	£270m — NEB (£370m approved)
1983-84	£100m from 1982, £100m — new funding, £25m — NEB

Source: Adapted from E. Cotterill and K. Boyfield, *BL: A Viable Future* (London, 1981) and S.Wilks, *Industrial Policy and the Motor Industry* (Manchester, 1984).

Table 1.3
British Leyland's Non-Commercial Vehicle Ranges, 1978 and 1981

1978	1981
Allegro	Acclaim
Dolomite	Ital
Jaguar Saloon	Jaguar Saloon
Marina	Maxi
Maxi	Metro
Mini	Mini
MG B	Princess
Midget	Range Rover
Princess	SD 1
Rover SD 1	TR 7
Rover 3500/s	XJS
Range Rover	
Spitfire	
Stag	
Triumph 2000/2500	
TR 7	
XJS	

Source: Various *SMMT Year Books.*

There is no doubt that Edwardes faced severe problems. While carrying through the programme of rationalisation, he also faced another consequence of BL's financial inadequacy. For the previous five years, funds had been too low to permit a satisfactory level of investment in new models, but the tired old existing designs were rapidly losing popularity. Short-term measures were needed until the firm could provide sufficient investment capital of its own. One of these measures, which turned out to have much longer-term consequences than Edwardes could have imagined, was a deal with Honda, whereby BL was to produce the Honda Ballade under licence as the Triumph Acclaim. Edwardes' most widely acknowledged achievement was the reduction of the power of the unions within the

Table 1.4
British Leyland's Models and Production Output, 1970 to 1994

Year	Production Volume	Number of Models Produced
1970	788,700	20
1971	886,721	22
1972	916,218	21
1973	873,839	22
1974	738,503	22
1975	605,141	22
1976	687,875	18
1977	651,069	17
1978	611,625	17
1979	503,767	15
1980	395,820	10
1981	398,763	11
1982	383,074	10
1983	445,364	8
1984	383,324	7
1985	465,104	7
1986	404,454	8
1987	471,504	7
1988	474,687	7
1989	466,619	8
1990	464,612	9
1991	395,624	9
1992	378,797	9
1993	406,804	11
1994	452,500[#]	10

Source: Various *SMMT Year Books*; [#]from BMW Annual Report and Accounts (1994).

Plate 1.1 Morris Assembly Line, Cowley, 1933

organisation.[25] By the time he left the company, in 1982, he believed he had returned power to the management by concentrating on new models.[26] Sir Graham Day, one of his successors, believed that the most important achievement of this period was to direct the firm towards the market place through the creation of new models, and to enable it to survive by improving productivity.[27]

Day's strategies for the company resembled those of Wilks half a century earlier, strategies which had lain dormant in the company all this time. They involved concentration on customer-targeted vehicles, matched to the aspirations of customers, rather than imitating products offered by competitors. This strategy, it was thought, would allow the company to charge more for its cars, leading to higher profit levels. Day continued Edwardes's policy of contracting the company to a 'base level'.[28] He also extended the collaboration with Honda, whilst trying to explore and capture niche sectors of the market. At the same time he sold many surplus facilities including the truck and bus businesses, Freight Rover and Jaguar, which had already been floated as a separate company in 1984.[29]

The modern Rover organisation emerged from the restructuring undertaken by Edwardes and followed up by Day. It was Day who re-established Rover as the trading name for the firm. Rover still owes much of its character to the rediscovered Rover heritage, but it also still exhibits characteristics of key parts of BMC and Leyland. Even after all the restructuring, the firm is still centred on three major manufacturing sites and the cultures of the predecessor organisations: Rover's Solihull, now home to Land Rover; the Austin works at Longbridge where small and medium sized car manufacturing is based, and Morris's Cowley works, remodelled by BL, for large car production. Each of these operations retains many traits from its own historical development which, along with the corporate Rover image, influences the strategies and performance of the firm.

At Solihull, where heavy engineering, low volume production, and slow evolution are the rule, the people in the factory still say they work at 'the Rover', harking back to the days of the P series Rover cars. The Land Rover culture, reflected in all areas of the organisation from the shop floor to the design office, is one of a privileged, skilled, craft-based organisation, which is able to contemplate changes at great length and develop carefully thought out plans to solve its problems. The Longbridge and Cowley approaches are quite different from the Solihull tradition, and have many similarities with each other. Both retain the traditional impulse of mass production, which regards volume of output as the supreme good. These organisations are great users of fresh ideas acquired from outside the factory walls; here there is no feeling, as there is at Land Rover, of superiority towards ideas developed outside the firm. Austin's Longbridge factory, where smaller cars are produced, has maintained some products of its own design, such as the Metro, and has its own new model centre working on possible future Rover small cars. This gives the site a sense of tradition; it is waiting to emerge from the shadow of the Japanese-derived Honda core products such as the R8 (Rover 200/400) and its replacement, project Theta (the 1995 Civic/Rover 400).

At Cowley, too, the ethos is very much that of mass production. The greatest rationalisation at Cowley took place under BL and early in Day's stewardship, with many models replaced by production centred on the site of the Pressed Steel Company and the BL body works. As a result the organisation is more in the spirit of the now departed BL Maestro and Montego models and the Honda-derived 800, rather than of the old, more highly respected, Morris, MG, Wolseley and Riley. The investment in the Rover 600 (which was essentially the 1994 Honda Accord) at Cowley gave it the most modern of Rover's facilities, but this investment alone was not enough to transform the prospects of the firm.

The sale of the company to BAe in January 1989 brought another change in leadership. Day was made chairman and replaced as CEO by George Simpson, from Leyland Trucks, who had a background as an accountant in many of the group's companies. This was the fourth change in leadership in seven years — probably not the kind of stability that Kay believes generates competitive success in the modern corporation! The policies of Simpson's leadership were many and varied, but never really became fully crystallised as an era in Rover's history, being overshadowed by the pressing operating decisions of BAe. The strategies of the Rover company before the arrival of BMW were largely a continuation of those developed by Day.[30] Simpson championed the introduction of the Breakthrough approach as a means of finding the right direction for the company.[31] Breakthrough is a goal-orientated strategy tool prescribed by the US management consultants Charles Smith and Associates (see Chapter 5 for an explanation). There had been a high degree of centralisation within the group under Day, with the Land Rover organisation and the duplicated functions of the Cowley and Longbridge manufacturing sites being combined. Simpson introduced a new Product Supply organisation (with a function that combined manufacturing and product design). In this way, the trend towards centralisation first seen in the pre-BLMC days was reversed. The introduction of business units — effectively financially independent plants with a large degree of autonomy — helped to foster the different cultures of the Land Rover, Austin and Cowley sites. The adoption of this structure has implications for BMW's strategic options: with the operating units of the firm isolated from each other, it should be easier to implement localised closures or expansion policies, such as the assimilation of Land Rover into BMW's core and the rationalisation of Rover's car business.

Improvements in the manufacturing capabilities of the firm were a necessary but not sufficient condition for commercial success. In an earlier period Rover had concentrated production and distribution in the home UK market but, as Table 1.5 shows, its standing in its home market has continued to decline in recent years. Corporate recovery plans once promised a different and better world for Rover, in which volume sales on the home market would underwrite strong financial performance. The results since 1981 have been disappointing. In 1981 the company's share of UK car registrations stood at 20 per cent, but by 1993 it had fallen to 13 per cent and in 1994 it was down to 11 per cent. The economics of the business is such that if Rover sells 11 per cent of 2 million new car registrations, it sells just 200,000 units and that means that the business cannot be financially viable even in a peak year.

The decision to produce desirable but more expensive vehicles to compete with the volume manufacturers has not improved the long-term stability of the company. The reported profit and loss statements from the firm misleadingly include capital acquired as a result of the restructuring. As Table 1.6 shows, the profits (or more appropriately the scale of the losses) at Rover have showed a slight improvement, but this includes much reduction in the assets of the firm. Injections of capital have come from sales: land to BAe; many supporting areas of the firm such as ISTEL (the systems development arm); and the

Table 1.5
Rover Group Share of UK Car Registrations

	New Car Registrations	Ford %	Rover %	Vauxhall %
1981	1,484,700	30.9	19.2	8.5
1982	1,555,000	30.5	17.8	11.7
1983	1,791,700	28.9	18.6	14.6
1984	1,749,647	27.8	17.8	16.1
1985	1,832,027	26.5	17.9	16.6
1986	1,882,474	27.4	15.8	15.1
1987	2,013,693	28.8	15.0	13.5
1988	2,215,574	26.4	15.0	13.7
1989	2,300,944	26.5	13.6	15.2
1990	2,008,934	25.2	14.0	16.1
1991	1,593,601	24.2	14.4	15.6
1992	1,539,106	22.2	13.5	16.7
1993	1,792,592	21.5	13.4	17.1

Source: K. Williams, C. Haslam and S. Johal, 'Who's Responsible? BAe: BMW: Honda: Rover' (unpublished paper, 22 February 1994).

profitable parts activities, such as Land Rover Parts. The profits reported in the last few years are in fact quite weak for a firm with such a large turnover, representing less than a 2 per cent return on sales. If Rover had not been helped by the government cancelling BAe's repayment of state aid given during the 1970s and 1980s, which is still being investigated by the European Union,[32] the accumulated losses would have forced the firm into bankruptcy many years ago.

Table 1.6
Profit and Loss at Rover, 1981-94

Year	Turnover (£M)	Profit (Loss)	Return on Sales	Accumulated Profit/Loss
1981	2,869	-503.7	n/a	-504
1982	3,072	-300.5	n/a	-804
1983	3,421	-142.9	n/a	-947
1984	3,402	80.6	2.4%	-867
1985	3,415	-138.0	n/a	-1,005
1986	3,412	-892.1	n/a	-1,897
1987	3,096	-26.8	n/a	-1,923
1988	1,179#	35.0	3.0%	-1,888
1989	3,430	64.0	1.9%	-1,824
1990	3,785	55.0	1.5%	-1,769
1991	3,744	-52.0	n/a	-1,821
1992	3,684	-49.0	n/a	-1,870
1993	4,301	56.0	1.3%	-1,814
1994	n/a	4.8*	n/a	-1,810

Sources: Company Reports and Accounts; #part year figure from BAe Report; *nine month figure from BMW Report.

Rover, then, received two lifelines, one from state ownership during the 1970s which enabled it to survive until a way of reversing its fortunes could be found; and another from the relationship with Honda. However, the new Rover, even with help from Honda, was not able to ensure its own survival. The reasons for BMW acquiring Rover and its reported capabilities are not immediately clear. The traditional view of a takeover as a means of market entry or defence does not fit the situation. BMW's rear-wheel-drive cars are already established in the UK, and the firm has the enviable record of being alone with Toyota in never having made a loss in the UK.[33] The draw of four-wheel-drive (4x4) and front-wheel-drive small cars could be explained in terms of market development strategies, but the takeover goes against the recent trend in the car industry, where some firms have formed joint ventures to spread the costs of model development. But what had Rover learnt from Honda that could entice BMW into spending £500m, particularly when Honda has cut the link so quickly?[34] The remaining chapters should provide some answers to this question.

Notes

1. C. Prahalad and G. Hamel, 'The Core Competence of the Corporation', *Harvard Business Review* (May-June 1990), pp. 79-91.
2. J. Womack, D. Jones and D. Roos, *The Machine that Changed the World* (London, 1990).
3. W. Lewchuk, *American Technology and the British Vehicle Industry* (Cambridge, 1987).
4. M.E. Porter, *Competitive Strategy: Techniques for Analyzing Industries and Competitors* (New York, 1980); idem, *The Competitive Advantage of Nations* (London, 1990).
5. A.D. Chandler, *Strategy and Structure: Chapters in the History of the American Enterprise* (Cambridge, MA, 1962); idem, *Scale and Scope: The Dynamics of Industrial Capitalism* (Cambridge MA, 1990).
6. J.B. Quinn, *Strategies for Change: Logical Incrementalism* (New York, 1980).
7. D. Miller and P. Friesen, *Organisations: A Quantum View* (New Jersey, 1984).
8. H. Mintzberg, *Structures in Fives: Designing Effective Organisations* (Englewood Cliffs, NJ, 1983).
9. Prahalad and Hamel, 'Core Competence'.
10. J. Kay, *Foundations of Corporate Success* (Oxford, 1993).
11. This study approach was developed in a series of papers including: H. Mintzberg and A. McHugh, 'Strategy Formulation in an Adhocracy', *Management Science Quarterly*, Vol. 31 (1985), pp. 160-97; H. Mintzberg, 'Patterns in Strategy Formulation', *Management Science*, Vol. 24 No. 9 (1978), pp. 934-48; H. Mintzberg and J. Waters, 'Tracking Strategy in an Entrepreneurial Firm', *Academy of Management Journal*, Vol. 25 No. 3 (1982), pp. 465-99; H. Mintzberg, 'Tracking Strategy in the Airlines: PWA, 1945-1985', *Canadian Journal of Administrative Science*, Vol. 3 No. 2 (1986), pp. 171-203; H. Mintzberg and J.Waters, 'Researching the Formation of Strategies: The History of Canadian Lady, 1939-76', in R. Lamb (ed.), *Competitive Strategic Management* (London, 1984).
12. See for example the long interview with Rover Managing Director John Towers by K. Eason, 'Rover's Return', Car 95 Supplement, *The Times*, 4 March 1995.
13. G. Robson, *The Rover Story* (Cambridge, 1984).
14. The trajectory of innovation in the cycle industry is analysed in W. Bijker, T. Hughes and T. Pinch, *The Social Construction of Technological Systems* (Cambridge MA, 1987); R. Roy, 'Design Evolution, Technological Innovation and Economic Growth', in R. Roy and D. Wield (eds.), *Product Design and Technological Innovation*

(Buckingham, 1986).
15. R. Whipp and P.A. Clark, *Innovation in the Auto Industry* (London, 1986).
16. R. Church, *Herbert Austin: The British Motor Car Industry to 1941* (London, 1979).
17. R. Overy, *William Morris, Viscount Nuffield* (London, 1976).
18. K. Richardson, *The British Motor Industry, 1896-1939* (London, 1977).
19. Ibid.
20. D. Ryder for Secretary of State for Industry, *British Leyland: The Next Decade* (The Ryder Report) (1975), pp. 11-12. Only the half-year figure is available as a result of the intervention of the government in December of 1974 and the subsequent restructuring of the firm's finances.
21. Ryder, *Next Decade*, p. 3.
22. Ibid., p. 17.
23. P. Dunnett, *The Decline of the British Motor Industry* (London, 1980), p. 133.
24. M. Edwardes, *Back From the Brink* (London, 1983), p. 95.
25. K. Williams, J. Williams and C. Haslam, *The Breakdown of Austin Rover* (Leamington Spa, 1987).
26. K. Starkey and A. McKinlay, 'Beyond Fordism? Strategic Choice and Labour Relations in Ford U.K.', *Industrial Relations Journal*, Vol. 20 No. 2 (1989), pp. 93-100.
27. G. Day in R. Heller (ed.), *The State of Industry, Can Britain Make It?* (London, 1987), p. 168.
28. G. Day, interview, March 1990.
29. J. Underwood, *The Will to Win: J. Egan and Jaguar* (London, 1989).
30. G. Simpson, interview, June 1990.
31. For a description of the breakthrough process and its adoption at Rover, see Chapter 5 and the case study in A. Pilkington, 'A Study of Strategy Formulation in an Automotive Manufacturer' (unpublished Ph.D. thesis, University of Aston in Birmingham, 1991, Ch. 7).
32. See for example M. Harrison, 'EC to Revive Rover Sweeteners Issue', *Independent*, 28 July 1992, p. 8.
33. Interview with BMW UK manager, Nov. 1994.
34. 'Honda puts Brake on Rover Ties and Reviews £400m Deals', *Independent*, 22 Feb. 1994, p. 1.

2

The Manufacturing Revolution

> *Manufacturing is the bones, the sinew and the muscles of the company. A healthy manufacturing function gives the company the strength to withstand competitive attack, it gives the endurance to maintain a steady improvement in competitive performance, and perhaps most important, it provides the operational suppleness which can respond to increasingly volatile markets and competitors.*[1]

This chapter explores the evolution of current best practice in the car industry, and enables a more informed estimate of the extent of the renewal which has taken place at Rover. Innovation in manufacturing and work methods has replaced quality and reliability as the source of competitive advantage in manufacturing industry. This has been most sharply felt in the automotive industry with the arrival of 'lean production' — a package of techniques which includes 'just in time' (JIT) and 'total quality management' (TQM). The need for European automotive producers to renovate their manufacturing operations in order to remain competitive has led to many new strategies and methods of organisation. Many have proved successful in the short term, in so far as the firms practising them have continued to exist. The fact remains, however, of overall Japanese supremacy. So what did the Japanese producers do to 'rejuvenate', as Abernathy put it,[2] the car industry?

Before attempting to answer this question, it is worth looking at early innovations in manufacturing. These can be traced back to the development of the production line at Ford's Highland Park and River Rouge plants in the 1920s, which set the pattern for the mass production of vehicles and other items throughout this century. It was competition from Ford that forced the early British car makers to adopt moving production lines during the 1920s.[3] A reworking of the

Fordist approach is occurring in the second half of the century as the world becomes aware of the activities in Japanese car assembly plants — and those of Toyota in particular. The rise of the Japanese car manufacturers to their present elevated position is shown in Table 1.1 above, which demonstrates how North American and UK production has stagnated since the 1960s, whereas Japanese output has more than tripled in the last 20 years.

Studies of the Japanese approach first appeared in the late 1970s and early 1980s. Abernathy,[4] Monden,[5] Ohno[6], Cusumano[7] and others compared the failure of the auto industry in the United States with the corresponding success of Toyota in Japan. Their findings were not taken up by the manufacturing community, with the exception of some progressive companies outside the motor industry and a few management consultants. The debate over the re-invention of car manufacture was reopened by the IMVP (International Motor Vehicle Programme) study, published as *The Machine that Changed the World*,[8] and associated texts from the other members of the research team.[9] This study investigated the state of the world auto industry, and its over-riding conclusion was that there was a generic operating method for Japanese firms, termed 'lean production', which was the model for future competition in the car industry. This finding is in fact an oversimplification; closer investigation of the lean production systems used at Toyota (that most closely followed in the IMVP study) and its closest competitors — Nissan, Honda and Mazda (see Table 2.1) — shows great variations in the ways lean manufacturers operate.

The success of Japanese car manufacturers has been attributed to lean production alone, without taking into account the specific strategies and approaches of the different firms. In the UK, however, there has been a debate concerning the novelty of the Japanese auto manufacturers' practices. Williams, Williams and Haslam[10] have contested the findings of the IMVP study, particularly the findings on production efficiency (shown in Table 2.2). Most interestingly, they map Henry Ford's factory on to the IMVP data, and find that by most measures the Toyota facilities lag behind their predecessor! For example, Ford had an inventory of two hours' stock between departments,[11] whereas today Toyota has around four hours. They, and others, also challenge the IMVP's claim that Japanese plants have a 2:1 efficiency advantage over their US counterparts: 'The

Table 2.1
World Auto Production in 1990 by Manufacturers (Ranked by Volume of Car Production)

Rank	Manufacturer	Cars	Commercial Vehicles	Total
1	General Motors — USA	5,208,221	1,936,335	7,144,556
2	Toyota — Japan	3,799,921	871,387	4,671,308
3	Ford — USA	3,703,646	1,831,639	5,535,285
4	Volkswagen — W. Germany	2,873,869	139,063	3,012,932
5	Peugeot/Citroen — France	2,459,139	241,916	2,701,055
6	Nissan — Japan	2,349,165	716,124	3,065,289
7	Fiat — Italy	1,805,449	263,873	2,069,322
8	Honda — Japan	1,764,775	160,322	1,925,097
9	Renault — France	1,666,434	321,973	1,988,407
10	Mazda — Japan	1,302,464	304,588	1,607,052
11	Mitsubishi — Japan	870,112	502,549	1,372,661
12	Chrysler — USA	859,245	954,048	1,813,293
13	VAZ — USSR	736,050	0	736,050
14	Hyundai — S. Korea	585,092	118,384	703,476
15	Daimler Benz — W. Germany	574,191	240,793	814,984
16	Suzuki — Japan	511,832	330,726	842,558
17	BMW — W. Germany	499,823	0	499,823
18	Rover — UK	464,612	63,195	527,807
19	Volvo — Sweden	377,878	61,559	439,437
20	Daihatsu — Japan	373,110	263,339	636,449
21	Fuji/Subaru — Japan	352,046	197,174	549,220
22	Alfa Romeo — Italy	223,643	0	223,643
23	Kia — S. Korea	222,125	174,200	396,325
24	FSM — Poland	203,642	0	203,642
25	Isuzu — Japan	202,347	395,336	597,683
26	Skoda — Czechoslovakia	187,181	0	187,181
27	Daewoo — S. Korea	184,795	16,240	201,035
28	Zastava — Yugoslavia	178,826	9,916	188,742

29	ZAZ Zaporojetz — USSR	155,620	0	155,620
30	GAZ Volga — USSR	138,100	0	138,100
31	Moskvitch — USSR	106,600	0	106,600
32	Trabant — E. Germany	91,893	0	91,893
33	Saab/Scania — Sweden	87,356	38,194	125,550
34	FSO — Poland	80,248	14,000	94,248
35	IMV — Yugoslavia	70,367	799	71,166
36	Wartburg — E. Germany	52,237	0	52,237
37	Sevel — Argentina	34,859	6,448	41,307
38	Porsche — W. Germany	32,162	0	32,162
39	Hino — Japan	0	100,417	100,417
40	Navistar — USA	0	78,591	78,591

Source: Motor Vehicle Manufacturers' Association of USA, *World Motor Vehicle Data* (Detroit, MI, 1992), p. 19.

Japanese industry's margin of superiority in physical or financial terms is relatively small and nowhere near 2:1'.[12] However, Toyota does have a labour productivity advantage of 30 per cent over its American rivals, ample justification for the interest in JIT and lean production.

Before describing the Japanese re-invention of car manufacturing, the various steps and processes involved in the manufacture of a vehicle need explaining (Figure 2.1). The heart of vehicle manufacture is the final assembly area, where many sub-assemblies and bought-out finished (BOF) parts (so termed, because the parts are bought in a finished state from an outside supplier, and not manufactured by the firm itself) are added to a painted steel body-shell to make the car. The start of the process, however, is in the press-shop, where sheet metal is stamped to produce body parts. These are then welded together to produce the body-shell. This area is often referred to as body-in-white, because the metal body is unpainted. The sequence of Plates, 2.1, 2.2 and 2.3, give examples of how this process has developed over the years — from wooden construction, through manual spot welding of sheet metal, to fully automated robotic body-framing lines. The white bodies are painted by dipping them into vats of primer and spraying with colour coats and sealants (Plate 2.4). They are dried in ovens before entering the final assembly hall.

Table 2.2
IMVP Summary of Assembly Plant Characteristics

	Japanese in Japan	Japanese in N.America	American	All Europe
Performance				
Productivity (hours/vehicle)	16.8	21.2	25.1	36.2
Quality (defects/100 vehicles)	60.0	65.0	82.3	97.0
Layout				
Space (sq. feet/vehicle/year)	5.7	9.1	7.8	7.8
Size of repair area (per cent of assembly)	4.1	4.9	12.9	14.4
Inventories (days)	0.2	1.6	2.9	2.0
Workforce				
% of workforce in teams	69.3	71.3	17.3	0.6
Job rotation (0=none, 4=often)	3.0	2.7	0.9	1.9
Suggestions/employee/year	61.6	1.4	0.4	0.4
Number of job classes	11.9	8.7	67.1	14.8
Training of new production workers (hours)	380.3	370.0	46.4	173.3
Absenteeism (per cent)	5.0	4.8	11.7	12.1
Automation				
Welding (% direct steps)	86.2	85.0	76.2	76.6
Painting (% direct steps)	54.6	40.7	33.6	38.2
Assembly (% direct steps)	1.7	1.1	1.2	3.1

Source: J. Womack, D. Jones and J. Roos, *The Machine that Changed the World* (New York, 1990), p .97.

Figure 2.1
Automotive Assembly Plant Production Process

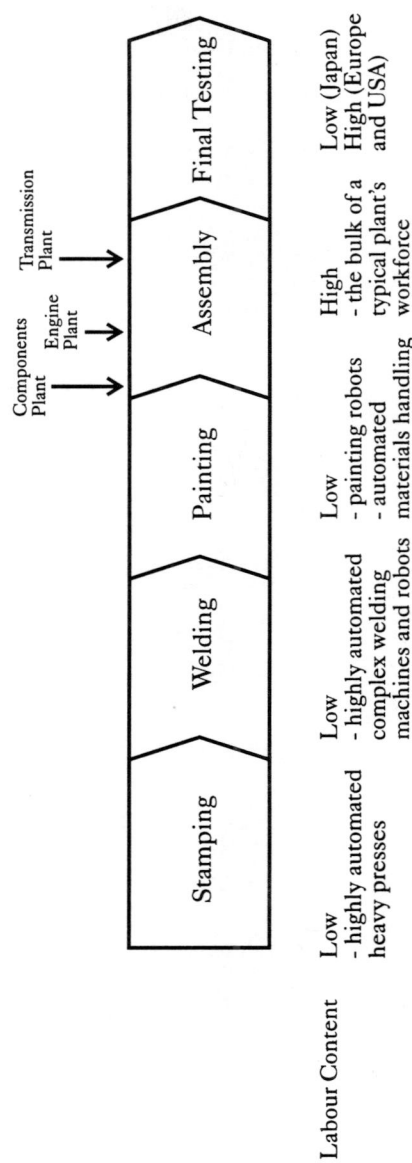

Source: *EIU International Motor Business* (1st quarter, 1994), p. 105.

Plate 2.2 The Mini Body-in-White Line of the 1970s, Longbridge

Plate 2.3 Robot Welding of the R8, Longbridge, 1990s

Plate 2.4 Automated Paint Spraying, Longbridge, 1990s

At the same time, elsewhere in the factory (or at a feeder plant), engines are being made on a production line — much like the final assembly line. Castings are machined and then assembled with other machined and BOF parts into complete engines. The gearbox undergoes the same process, with gears assembled into casings. The engine and gearbox are then mated together to give a single power unit ready for assembly with the rest of the vehicle in a single operation in the final assembly hall (Plate 2.5). Most of the parts of a modern car are not manufactured by the car producers, but are bought from outside specialists. Thus 50 to 80 per cent of the value of a modern car is accounted for by BOF components, completed by other firms, and delivered in bulk to the assembly lines. By contrast, only 40 per cent of the earlier Ford cars consisted of BOF parts.[13] The move towards buying out parts, instead of manufacturing them (vertical integration), was one of Morris's innovations, developed as a means of minimising the need to invest in machinery.[14]

Abernathy's description of innovation in the car industry and the way in which the US lagged behind the Japanese provides a very powerful illustration of how production methods developed, and provides an insight into the pioneering work of the Japanese in lean production.[15] Abernathy's list of major innovations is shown in Table 2.3. It should be remembered that Abernathy was concentrating on the US car industry, where the styles of vehicles differ from those in Europe and Japan, but the message from the list is quite clear: most advances in American vehicle production, since Ford, have been advances in the design of the vehicles, not in their manufacture. It is the manufacturing process itself that Toyota and its domestic rivals have revolutionised in the last 30 years.

The revolution can be best explained by considering in some detail the following seven elements of post-Japanese (or more correctly post-Toyota) car manufacture: manufacturing philosophy, design process, total quality management, flow layout, maintenance, *kanban* and supply chain management. These are the factors which have dominated thinking at Rover in its bid to become a lean producer.

1. Manufacturing Philosophy

There is great variety in the way Japanese organisations have approached lean production. Toyota concentrates on reducing waste in the company,[16] and has taken 40 years to develop the Toyota production system — the blueprint for JIT. Toyota has extended the waste reduction philosophy into other manufacturing activities ranging from sewing machines to pre-fabricated buildings. The Toyota JIT system is called, paradoxically, 'batch-of-one' production. The waste reduction philosophy refines the process of mass production to the point that the company operates its production facilities to make single units matching customer orders; most customers buy just one vehicle at a time. Honda have similarly aspired to efficiency and waste reduction, but the driving force in the company is the belief of founder Soichiro Honda that the design of the vehicles is paramount to customer satisfaction.[17] Honda concentrates on removing variations in the manufacturing process to ensure that the vehicle conforms to product standards. This is achieved by producing vehicles in large batches, not batch-of-one as at Toyota, and designing the production line around the notion of optimally small batch sizes — the smallest number Honda believes it can make efficiently and, more importantly, consistently. Repetition is seen as the key to producing something correctly. The Honda Concerto production line, as supplied to Rover for the R8 (from 1990 onwards, Rover 200 and 400 models), is an integrated facility producing batches of 90 vehicles identical in three respects — model-territory-option (MTO). These can then be divided at the point of final assembly into three batches of 30 to be painted, each in its own colour. Thus the three batches of 30 are defined by model-territory-option-colour (MTOC). The colour does not affect the work content of the vehicle, and batching in this way makes the paint process more efficient and easier to manage; there are fewer change-overs in paint colour which necessitate the flushing out of unused paint in the paint guns. In practice, the normal batch size processed on this facility by Honda in its Ohio, USA plant is 150 MTOC, much larger than the 30 MTOC minimum; this ensures greater consistency and manufacturing efficiency.

Mazda has yet another approach to lean production which is reflected in the company's aim to be highly flexible, even at the cost of some loss of efficiency. Mazda decided that the best method of gaining advantage against larger rivals was to build mixed-models on one production facility.[18] The normal approach, as adopted at Toyota

Table 2.3
Abermathy's Chronicle of Innovations in the Auto Industry

Innovation	Source	Date	Details
Disc brakes	Lanchester (GB)	1904	More consistent than drum brakes and resistant to water, etc.
Aluminium alloy piston	Corbin and Cie	1915	Lightweight pistons which distribute the heat quicker than steel
Closed steel body	Budd	1921	Earlier vehicles had no roof and were wooden; the closed steel bodies were mass produced
Welded body assembly	Budd	1925	Riveting was replaced by faster, more economical, welding
Cemented carbide tools	Krupp	1928	Extended tool life and cutting speeds improve productivity
Automatic choke	AC (GB)	1931	Convenient, improved engine performance and longer life
Independent front suspension	Amedee Bolle (F)	1933	Improved safety, handling and ride by isolating the axles
Cast crank and camshafts	Ford	1934	Lower weight and cheaper to produce than forged shafts
High compression V8 engine	Otto (D)	1934	Improved efficiency of large American cars
Unit body construction	Vauxhall (GB)	1935	Monocoque or stressed skin removing the need for a separate chassis
Automatic transmission	Sturtevant	1937	Very popular in America but less influential in Europe to date

Innovation	Source	Date	Details
Integration of engine plants	Smith for GM	1947	Repetitive nature of engine manufacture made this the first area to benefit from transfer lines and robotics
Computer-assisted scheduling	GM	1950	Production scheduling improves efficiency and cuts inventories
Energy absorbing steering	?	1956	Safety feature prevents injury to the driver
Electrical system advances	?	1956	Maintenance-free ignition systems and more electrical accessories powered by 12 volt system
Dip painting and electrocoat	AMC	1963	Submerging an electrically charged body into the paint attracts the primer evenly over the surface, limiting corrosion and reducing waste of spray painting
Auto chassis & body assembly	?	1966	Use of more complex robotic technology than in engine manufacture for the production of body in white
Programmable logic control	?	1972	Easily reprogrammable relays control limited production automation
Aluminium engine	Haynes	1985	Light-weight, heat-conducting and cheap to machine, are only now widely available

Source: W.J. Abernathy, *The Productivity Dilemma: Innovation in the Automobile Industry* (Baltimore, MD, 1978), Appendix 2.

Plate 2.5 The Robotic Glazing Cell in R8 Final Assembly, Longbridge, 1990s

and Honda, is to design a production line to make one type or model of car. If the complexity of the process is increased to accommodate more than one model, the risks involved, and the complexity of managing such a facility, make the whole process inefficient. Mazda's latest production lines are designed to build 15 models on one line. This approach is an extension of the Toyota JIT system, which allows any MTOC to be built as batch-of-one within the model range. Mazda's system has the potential to provide the same batch-of-one, but the car can be any MTOC from any of the 15 different models produced by the facility. This reduces the company's break-even volume for new models, which Mazda can then direct towards certain niche markets, and not concern itself with satisfying the wider mass markets. This strategy can be seen in recent Mazda models, like the MX5, which have re-created markets for small, inexpensive sports cars, a market which other manufacturers have decided cannot economically sustain mass produced models.

So how does this stand against the IMVP notion of lean production as a well-defined approach adopted throughout the Japanese car industry? Honda is definitely lean in its operations but does not follow Toyota's batch-of-one production. Mazda is also lean by Western standards, but has chosen to sacrifice some leanness to be flexible enough to meet the demands of customers who are likely to shift from one model to another. The variation in manufacturing philosophy reflects the differing impact of market forces on the companies: volume of sales, past experiences and the different capabilities of the organisations. Toyota occupies a dominant position in the market and sells in large volumes — hence production efficiency is a key strategy. Honda has a historical reason for its approach to leanness, whilst Mazda's low volume niche market products have led it to mixed-model production.

2. Design Process

The manufacturing developments of the lean producers have given them advantages in efficiency over their Western rivals, who have traditionally concentrated on product development to generate competitive advantages. Car design has become remarkably convergent in the 1980s, as standardised aerodynamics often make it difficult to tell European models apart. Many small innovations in car design have been adopted by nearly all manufacturers over the years, but none has had the impact that the lean production approach has had upon the manufacturing practices and company organisation of the car makers. Abernathy studied the pre-lean innovations whilst investigating the competitiveness of the US car industry — his findings are summarised in Table 2.3 — but none of these radically changed the basis of competition in the world auto industry in the way that the activities of the Japanese manufacturers have. Recent design features established in European cars include anti-lock braking systems, whereby the steering can still function, and the driver retain control, under heavy braking. Similarly, advertising copy is full of vehicles offering air-bags, which inflate on impact preventing serious injury, but which deflate almost instantly, allowing the driver to retain control of the car — Volvo even offers side air-bags, which spring from the side of the seat to prevent injury.

The biggest innovation in car design from Japan was not in the product itself but in the speeding up of the process of product design. The lean manufacturers build incremental design potential into their products so that new models are often little more that modifications of existing models, rather than completely new products. This seemingly allows a re-design of the car every five years. Traditional approaches were built on model replacement cycles of ten years (see Table 2.4). Accelerating the product development cycle feeds the consumer desire to own the newest model. New model launches in the car industry are a risky time. If a launch is successful, it leads to a surge in sales for the company's other products, but if the launch fails, the company's standing in the market place can suffer substantial damage — Ford lost ground for several years due to the initially poor reception of the Sierra. By replacing models more frequently, the damage caused by a poor launch can be reduced. Similarly, rapid product development can create a reputation for the company as an innovator, even if the changes in the product are small and basically cosmetic.

Accelerating the design cycle is achieved through a process called simultaneous engineering (also known variously as design for manufacture, concurrent engineering, parallel engineering and overlapping problem solving).[19] The simultaneous approach, which is described by Clark and Fujimoto,[20] involves removing the boundaries between product development and manufacturing activities. The

Table 2.4
Comparisons of Product Development in Japan and the West

	USA	Europe	Japan
Car sales (millions) — 1985	10.9	9.5	3.1
Car sales (millions) — 1975	8.3	7.6	2.7
Car imports % share 1985	28%	16% (EC)	2%
Average major model change interval (1982-87)	8.1 years	12.2 years	4.6 years
Development lead time (months)			
— average	61.9	57.6	42.6
— minimum	50.2	46.0	35.0
— maximum	77.0	70.0	51.0
Engineering hours (millions)	3.5	3.4	1.2
Body types (number) (product complexity)	1.7	2.7	2.3
Supplier engineering (% of total hours)	14%	36%	52%

Source: Adapted from K. Clark and T. Fujimoto, *Product Development Performance: Strategy, Organisation, and Management in the World Auto Industry* (Boston, MA, 1991), pp. 40, 73.

traditional view is that design is a task for design engineers — specialists working in secret away from the manufacturing plant. When the product engineers have finalised the design, it is passed on to manufacturing engineers to develop the manufacturing process and facilities. The simultaneous approach allows both sets of engineers to work together, so that both aspects of the project develop as one process (see Figure 2.2). If the manufacturing engineering staff are involved from the start of the project they are likely to detect errors of design which would later prove costly, or even impossible, to rectify.

The main point about innovation in car design, according to Gardiner,[21] is one of timing: some early design decisions tend to limit future possibilities while others expand them. Designs which can be extended are called robust, and spread the initial development costs over many future models. This technique has been used extensively

Figure 2.2
The Effect of Simultaneous Engineering on Product Development

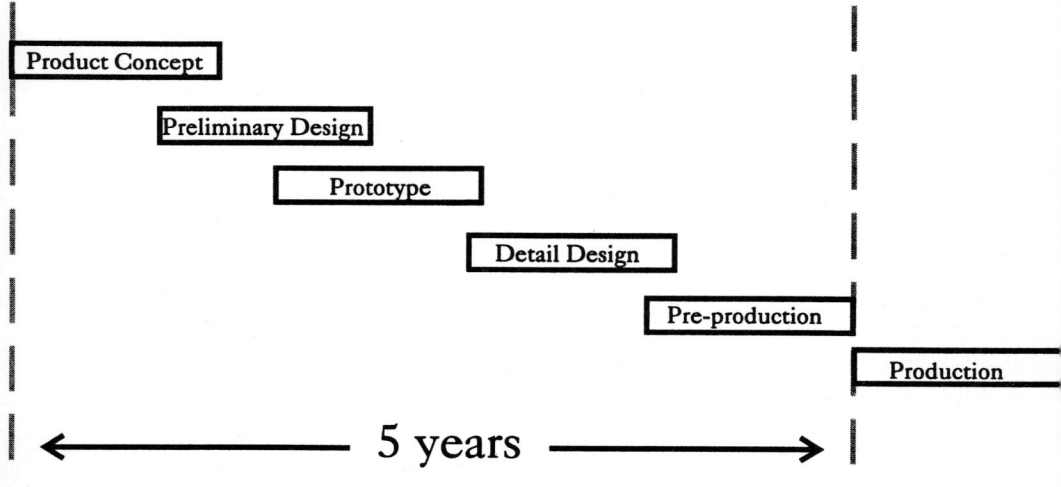

Western Model of Product Design Process

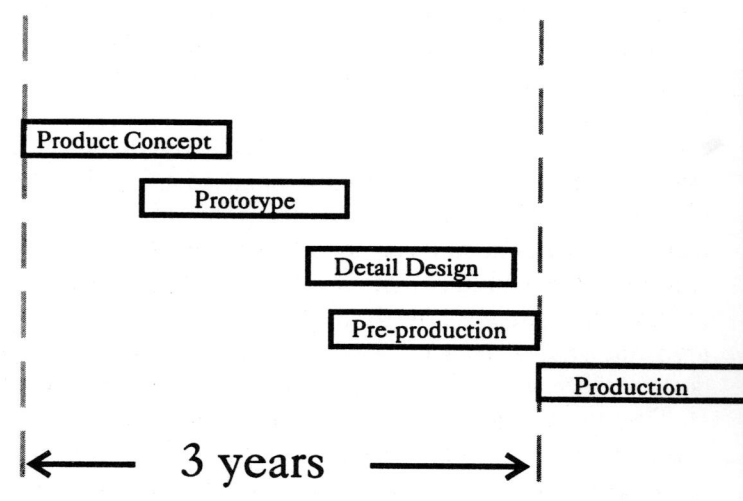

Simultaneous Engineering Product Design Process

by the Japanese car manufacturers, and is called part 'carry-over'. The work needed and time taken in model development can be cut dramatically if existing parts are used in the design of new products — it is not necessary to redesign the car from scratch. At Rover, the amount of carry-over design in a typical vehicle before the introduction of Honda never exceeded 50 per cent, but since the arrival of Honda this has increased to nearly 80 per cent and cut the development time by 30 per cent.[22]

The lean producers have also been the champions of techniques developed in the West, but not taken up by the manufacturers there. The adapting of Western methods is one of the most striking findings of Cusumano's study of Toyota and Nissan.[23] Cusumano argued that Japanese firms had not themselves developed innovative products; they had simply taken the best practices found in the West and tailored them for the demanding and consumer-focused Japanese market and maintained a diligent search for ways of cutting costs.

Avoiding complexity to achieve manufacturing efficiency is another maxim of lean production. The drive to satisfy customers has come a long way since Henry Ford proclaimed that the customer must be satisfied with a black model T. The need to provide customers with what they want, can cause many redundant elements to influence a design, as, for example, making provision for air conditioners and electric windows, even though these options account for only five per cent of production. Redundancy can add material and production costs to a manufacturer which eat into profit margins. An exercise in complexity analysis on a Rover 800 found that the customer was being invited to choose one out of a possible 186 million different cars.[24] Honda's version of this joint development programme, the Legend, was designed and marketed in only 163 different variations. No reduction of customer satisfaction after the rationalisation was detectable. As a result, Rover was able to redevelop its market pitch and offer limited option combinations, sold as packages, rather than encouraging the customer to pick from an *à la carte* menu. Reducing the complexity of both design and manufacturing strengthened the company's position in the eyes of customers (who had formerly become lost in the maze of options available), allowed the material costs of the car to be reduced, and simplified the manufacturing system.

The extreme case of the Rover 800 highlights the issue of

complexity in car manufacture. The lean producers have used its management to their advantage. The lean approach is to keep to a minimum options which have to be built into the car at an early stage in manufacture, while encouraging varying and hence differentiating features to be added at a later stage in the production process. As a result, the customer has plenty of choice, and the manufacturing operation is easier to manage. An example would be the selection of a variant which would necessitate the fitting of alloy wheels. The pre-lean approach would involve changing the suspension components to alter the height if different wheels and low profile tyres were fitted. In the lean process, the alloy wheels would require the same suspension settings as the ordinary wheels, or the adjustment would be of a kind that could be performed without having to replace any of the parts. Managing complexity in this way reduces the number of parts held in the factory, thereby cutting stocks and also reducing the risk that the wrong part might be fitted.

3. Total Quality Management

Lean design makes good use of 'Japanese management' techniques, which were adopted after the war from US consultants and quality experts like Demming and Juran. These approaches have become known collectively as Total Quality Management (TQM) and are used extensively in the lean company. TQM has been very popular in the USA and Europe since the 1980s, and nearly every progressive company has adopted it. TQM is difficult to describe concisely since it encompasses many different tools and techniques; however, its essence is that all the employees in the company or organisation are trained to monitor their own performance. In this way an organisation can mobilise its employees to ensure that all activities are carried out in a quality-conscious manner; the definition of quality used in manufacturing organisations is not one of luxury or prestige, but of fitness for purpose or conformity to standards.

Harrison identifies the elements of TQM as: the prevention and detection of mistakes, management leadership, integration of effort, and the ownership and continuous improvement of processes.[25] TQM, as summarised in Demming's 14 principles,[26] is a departure from the traditional management of quality by control. It needs leadership from executives to ensure consistency, and direction for future aims and goals. Leadership is also required to ensure that the different efforts of employees and organisational functions pull in the same direction in an integrated way. This approach is highly evident in TQM implementations where the first step for employees is to identify their customers and suppliers in the organisation. Once the links between different jobs and departments have been made clear, quality activities can be tailored to ensure that the needs of the other departments are met, effectively breaking down barriers to communication. This can be problematic when companies with a long tradition of compartmentalisation and division of labour introduce TQM. The rivalry between groups of employees, which may well have become ingrained over many years, needs to be broken down.

Proponents of TQM pay much attention to early detection and prevention of quality problems. It obviously costs less to invest in robust systems that are failsafe than to spend money correcting problems once they have occurred. *Poka-yoke*, translated from the Japanese as fault-proofing,[27] uses simple devices to ensure that errors cannot be made, such as steering wheels with locating pins which can only be fitted on to the steering column in one way and not at an angle as can happen with an hexagonal or square mounting. Early detection of quality problems is carried out using techniques like statistical process control (SPC). SPC uses control charts to record and measure the performance of a process or operation. Employees take samples of the output from a process, and perform some simple analysis to calculate the average and range of the sample. These data are then plotted on the chart. If the data lie outside certain predetermined control limits, there is a statistical possibility that the process is not conforming to the desired standard and some remedial action may be necessary. If the reading is normal, the process is left alone. SPC monitoring can be applied to almost any activity or process in an organisation and, once it is set up, requires very little time or money to operate.

Once quality problems are identified, the TQM organisation concentrates on determining the cause and preventing the problem ever happening again. Simple problem-solving techniques are used, such as the cause-and-effect diagram, often called fishbone or Ishikawa diagrams after the Japanese professor who pioneered its introduction in the 1940s. The Ishikawa diagram is a way of logging a problem on to a chart which lists the possible reasons for failure or error. The rapid matching of problem with cause speeds up the search for a solution. Brainstorming (generating ideas from 'fact-holders'[28] in the organisation) and pareto analysis (prioritising the areas of concern) are an integral part of the cause-and-effect diagram.[29] Toyota has a useful approach to finding the cause of a quality problem: employees are encouraged to ask the question WHY? five times. This is usually sufficient to discover the cause of the problem, which can then be addressed to ensure that the error does not happen again.

The use of TQM techniques in the West has been dogged by a lack of commitment to training in some organisations[30] which erroneously see the expense not as an integral part of their operation, but as an overhead which can be reduced without affecting output. But training is only one of the steps towards ensuring that ownership of a processes resides with the person carrying it out. This is a departure from the traditional approach, where responsibility rests not with the operator, but with the section manager or some distant person in the quality control department. *Kaizen*[31] is another technique which is often used by TQM. It seeks to motivate the individuals in the organisation, not only to take responsibility for their part in the overall process, but also to develop ways of improving it. The sum of small improvements accruing throughout the firm can lead to a jump in the firm's performance and efficiency.

4. Flow Layout

The benefits of TQM alone do not account for the total productivity advantage of lean production. Much of the productivity advance comes from JIT, through material control and supply chain management. One of the most prohibitive aspects of introducing JIT is having to produce in batch-of-one rather than the economic batch quantity which prevailed under mass production.[32] In a world-class car factory, this means that the machines to produce a part have to be capable of making individual items within the typically one minute production cycle. This not only includes making the part, but also setting up the machine. Achieving fast set-ups can be prohibitively expensive, requiring major investments in new technology and equipment for handling material. For some parts, the aim of batch-of-one cannot be achieved, normally because of cycle-time constraints, but the batch sizes produced in lean factories are still much smaller than those set up on mass production lines. Shingo describes how the set-up times of press tools in the body-in-white area were reduced over several years, from many hours to just the press of a single button.[33] Most of the techniques reported by Shingo do not rely on technological solutions but simply on studying the problem carefully and organising the work effectively. The time taken to set up presses can be greatly reduced by standardising the last and normally most time-consuming stage, the final adjustment of the tool height to produce quality parts. Similar sized tools and dies are grouped together and only used on the same machine. In this way the settings needed to complete the final set-up can be quickly repeated. In the West, the approach has been to use the press tools and dies on all machines to maximise through-put efficiency — the belief being that by producing parts on any available machine, the work in the press shop could be spread out more evenly and the plant could operate more efficiently. But using the tools and dies in this way means that time-consuming final adjustments have to be repeated from scratch every time, producing many scrap pieces before a batch of good panels can be produced. The JIT approach stresses the importance of reducing the set-up time as far as possible so the total down-time (the time spent not producing) of the press lines can be reduced, even though the number of machine change-overs can increase a hundred-fold. The number of scrap panels produced during the set-up process is likewise very much reduced.

Improved set-up times help to increase the flexibility of the production system as a whole. Traditionally, different but similar parts were made on different specialist machines in order to achieve maximum levels of efficiency. Different types of wheels, for example, are made on different machines specially designed to make either steel or alloy wheels. In the JIT factory, having specialised machines for only a few parts is seen as wasteful, and the parts are therefore grouped together into families of parts and produced on multi-functional machines. A machine can then produce individual parts as required by the final production line and at maximum efficiency. If all wheels, for example, come from the same production cell, it does not matter whether they are alloy or steel. In the West, however, the alloy wheel production facility will be designed to produce at the average rate of alloy wheel usage by the final assembly line. It becomes a major issue of line balancing and production management if the mix of vehicles changes and the type of wheel has to be changed too. A lean factory only has to worry about volume changes and not changes in mix.[34]

The layout of the JIT factory also differs from a mass production facility because of its need to facilitate the flow of material in batches of one. Any time spent waiting for material to be delivered from one operation to the next is wasted and increases the pressure on maintaining batch-of-one. JIT facilities are therefore designed to reduce waiting and movement times. Instead of keeping the various work elements in each production operation separate, groups of production operations and workers are formed into cells. The cells assume responsibility for most aspects of production, from job assignment to housekeeping, enabling the introduction of TQM working. One extreme form of this organisation is the U-shaped cell. By laying out the machines in an operation in a U-shape it is possible to reduce the space needed and, more importantly, the distance the operator has to walk to complete the entire operation. In a traditional straight production line the employee has to walk back down to the start of the work-station to begin the next production cycle. In contrast, within a U-shape the operator effectively walks around a loop and, after having completed the last operation, is back at the start again to make the next part. This reduces the time needed to complete an operation. The U-shaped cell is a very efficient layout and is increasingly changing the design of factories, not only in the car industry.

5. Maintenance

The need for flexible and responsive production facilities has caused some problems in the development of JIT, such as how to ensure the reliability of production. In traditional car manufacture there was a tendency to have specialised maintenance engineers fully trained in looking after the production facilities. If there was a breakdown the procedure was to wait for the engineers to come and fix it. Excess stocks were used to keep the rest of the production line supplied while the machine was repaired. JIT does not have these safety stocks, so the reliability of machines becomes paramount. Preventive and operator-based maintenance programmes are a major feature of JIT factories, and have come to be known as TPM (total productive maintenance).[35] TPM improves the overall equipment effectiveness (OEE) by preventing losses due to breakdown, long set-up times, speed losses[36] and losses from defects resulting from poorly maintained machines. A typical TPM programme introduces similar steps to TQM: maintenance by the operator (from simple cleaning to training in set-up procedures), planned and preventive maintenance (regular machine servicing and the use of statistical techniques to predict what is likely to fail, and replace it before it does).

6. Kanban

The control of material in a JIT system has been well documented and hinges on the kanban system. *Kanban* is often translated as the Japanese word for ticket or request, but more accurately is a sign or advertisement. The *kanban* system uses a series of signals which pull material through the production system to replace material which has been used further down the production line. Before lean systems were introduced, the control of material was carried out to a regular schedule. Material flowed (or was pushed) through the production facilities to arrive at the final assembly whether it was needed or not. *Kanban* helps the JIT system to reduce waste, because only what has been used is replaced. When an operation uses a piece of material, this is effectively an instruction for replacements to be made. The *kanban* system is easy to implement if fast set-up times and flow processes have been established, but, if they have not, *kanban* (and so JIT) is nearly impossible to introduce because it takes too long to produce the replacement parts in response to the demands of the controlling final assembly line. Then, in order to make the *kanban* work the parts have to be batched together, which leads to increased storage space and costs.

7. The Supply Chain

It is no use just having the sub-assembly operations in the factory responding in small batches if the material suppliers are still delivering against forecast schedules in large quantities — the stocks of materials still exist and need funding. In a JIT system the deliveries to the factory also work in small batches. The suppliers are generally located close to the factory in order to meet the fast delivery times demanded by manufacturers. High quality levels are also demanded by the purchaser, there being no slack time in the JIT system for the delays which might result from necessary rectification, or waiting for another delivery if one is scrapped. In consequence, the suppliers and the purchaser, or original equipment manufacturer (OEM), have built up close relationships over many years. Lamming has developed a model representing the different stages of development which lead to a relationship of the type Toyota has with its suppliers (Table 2.5). This model shows how the traditional, true, supply-dominated buyer-seller relationship was forced by recessionary pressures into a more stressed relationship, with the buyer demanding more and more from the supplier, and the contract itself being re-negotiated in an annual bidding session. The negative aspects of this focus on price forced the Japanese approach to the fore, with more negotiation and building of long-term trust for mutual benefit. The belief is that there is unnecessary waste in working with someone who does not know how you work, or cannot be relied upon to deliver products of a consistent quality.

The structure of purchasing relationships in the car industry in Japan is quite different from those in the West. Instead of playing one supplier off against another to beat the price down, as happens annually in the West, the Japanese approach is to build price reductions, accrued from increases in efficiency, into long-term contractual relationships. The supplier companies are also involved in designing the parts they are to make — after all, they are going to have to make them — and therefore add an extra, well qualified, resource to the design team. In the West such an approach would be seen as a danger to confidentiality, since many UK suppliers are big firms working with several manufacturers. But the Japanese approach has led to a high degree of vertical disintegration and a heavily tiered structure in the supply base (see Figure 2.3). The close links are only with the first layer of the supply network, which in turn purchase units and components from general manufacturers and subcontractors, which in their turn use smaller firms to outsource work and supply part-finished materials for assembly. In the Western model, however, the first-tier suppliers (such as Lucas or Delco) generally manufacture the components in their entirety, obtaining only their raw materials from outside. It has been argued

Figure 2.3
The Structure of the Japanese Auto Supply Network

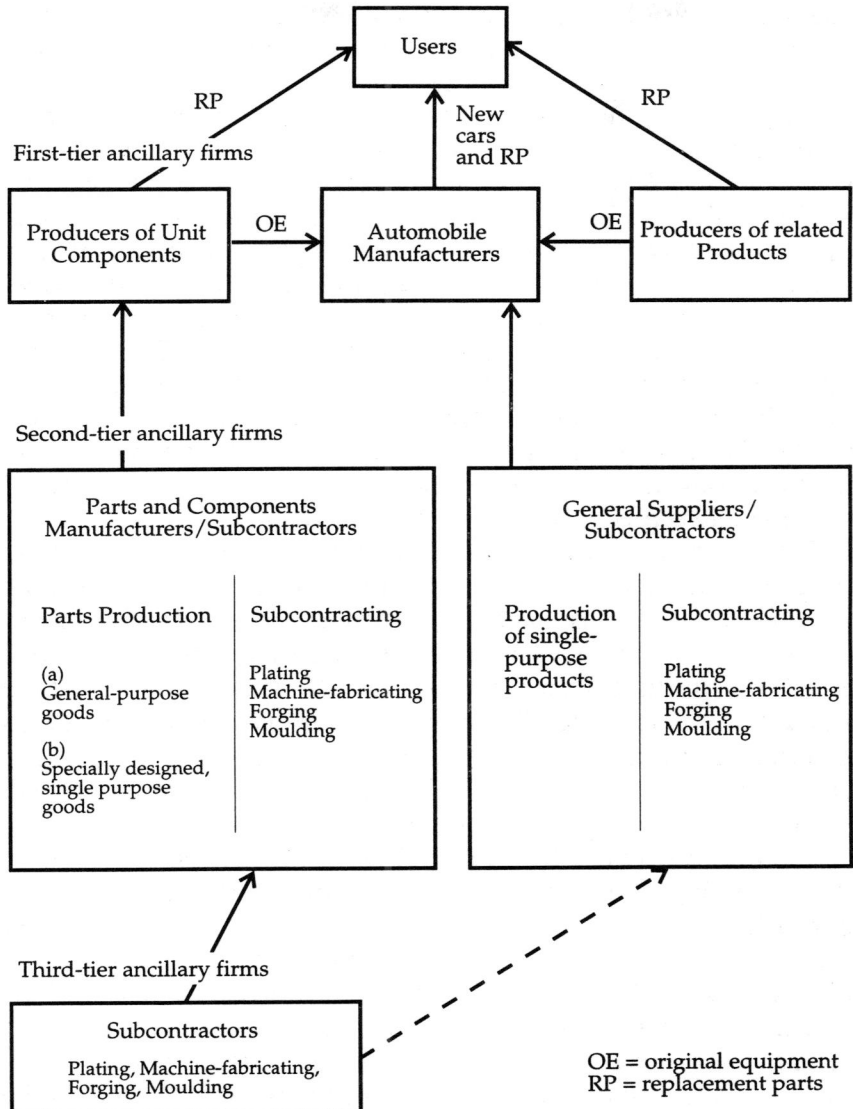

R. Morales, *Flexible Production: Restructuring of the International Automobile Industry* (Cambridge, MA, 1994).

Table 2.5
The Four Phase Model of Supplier Relationships

Model	Nature of Competition	Basis of Sourcing Decisions	Role of Data Exchange	Management of Capacity
Traditional: before 1975	Closed but friendly; plenty of business	Wide; enquiries; lowest bid; price-based	Very restricted, minimum necessary	Few problems: some poor scheduling
Stress: 1972-85	Closed and deadly, chaotic	'Dutch auctions', price-based	A weapon, one-way, supplier must open books	Spasmodic, no system to deal with chaos
Resolved: 1982 onwards	Closed, some collaboration, strategic	Price, quality and delivery	Two-way, short-term eg. forward building	Gradually improving, linkages appearing
Partnership/ Japanese: 1990 onwards	Collaboration, tiering, still dynamic	Performance history, long-term source, costs	Two-way, long-term, knowledge of costs	Co-ordinated and jointly planned

Table 2.5 (continued)

Delivery Practice	Dealing with Price Changes	Attitude to Quality	Role of R&D	Level of Pressure
Large quantities, buyer's choice, steady	General negotiation (annual); a game, win/lose	Inspection: arguments/ laissez-faire	One-sided: either assembler or supplier	Low/ medium, steady, predictable
Unstable, no control, variable, no notice of changes	Conflict in negotiation, a battle, lose/lose	Aggressive campaigns, SQA, etc.	Shared, but only for cost reductions	High/ unbearable, volatile
Smaller quantities, buyer's demands stabilising	Annual economics plus negotiation, win/lose	Joint effort towards improvement	Shared for development	Medium, some sense of relief
Small quantity, agreed basis, dynamic (JIT)	Annual economics plus planned reductions, win/win	Joint planning for development	Shared, some black or grey box	Very high, predictable

Source: R. Lamming, *Beyond Partnership: Strategies for Innovation and Lean Supply* (London, 1993), p. 152.

that this is a socially undesirable feature of the Japanese car industry; costs are passed on to small back-street firms which employ casual staff at reduced rates and accommodate the changing demand of the second-tier suppliers. This exploitative practice is impossible with highly integrated first-tier suppliers as in Europe.

Japanese policy is to have as far as possible one supplier for all related, though not identical parts. All wheels, for example, should come from a single supplier, not from different specialist wheel makers in alloy or steel as happens in the UK (see Table 2.6). The strategy of having a single supplier is necessary for JIT, in order to cope with the changes in product mix, all of which need to be accommodated in the production-delivery cycle-time. If there is a shift from one part in a family to another, the effect on a Western company is that the output from one supplier is turned off and another turned on. This kind of switch in demand can be disastrous for the supplier company, unless, as in the Japanese model, it also makes the other part being demanded.

Table 2.6
Suppliers to Major Car Manufacturers, 1988

Assembler	No. of Direct Suppliers (domestic supply)	Vehicles Built (domestic production: includes commercial vehicles)
Japan		
Toyota	340	3,968,697
Nissan	310	2,213,506
Honda	310	1,293,416
USA/Canada		
GM	2,500	5,876,013
Ford	1,800	3,982,209
Chrysler	2,000	2,207,104

Europe

Fiat	900	1,880,856
Renault	1,050	1,680,636
PSA	900	2,017,508
VW/Audi	1,580	1,879,748
D Benz	1,650	698,600
BMW	1,420	442,776
Porsche	600	25,969
Rover	850	520,299
Jaguar	540	51,939
Volvo	590	331,218
Saab	485	152,406

Source: R. Lamming, *Beyond Partnership: Strategies for Innovation and Lean Supply* (London, 1993), p. 172.

The pressures on Western car makers to compete with the new methods and approaches coming from Japan have proved irresistible. All firms have developed or adopted strategies to become more Japanese. Ford UK have its 'After Japan' programme, GM have entered into a joint-venture with Toyota in the US called New United Motor Manufacturing Inc. (NUMMI), and many of Rover's strategies detailed in this book, including the collaboration with Honda described in the next chapter, are prompted by the need to compete or go under. The European Union has also started a programme under its DG IV office, called 'Brite Euram', to try to determine how the European motor industry can address the new methods and remain competitive. The companies involved in Brite Euram include Rover, BMW, Mercedes, PSA (Peugeot Citroen Group), Renault, and Fiat. Ford and GM Europe, though not European-owned, have associate membership.

The ground rules for competition in manufacturing have been radically altered as a result of the development of the Japanese motor industry. Established levels of flexibility were extended, but with an efficiency close to that shown by the highly integrated Ford factories of the 1930s. There has, however, been a lack of finesse in many of the descriptions of what the new ground-rules are. Many accounts assume a general model of lean production for all the new leaders in the industry without considering the different approaches and the benefits which these bring.

Notes

1. N. Slack, *The Manufacturing Advantage* (London, 1991), p. 1.
2. W.J. Abernathy, *The Productivity Dilemma: Roadblock to Innovation in the Automobile Industry* (Baltimore, MD, 1978).
3. R. Church, *Herbert Austin: The British Motor Car Industry to 1941* (London, 1979), p. 84.
4. Abernathy, *Productivity Dilemma*.
5. Y. Monden, The *Toyota Production System* (Norcross, GA, 1983).
6. T. Ohno, *The Toyota Production System* (Tokyo, 1978).
7. M.A. Cusumano, *The Japanese Automobile Industry: Technology and Management at Nissan and Toyota* (Cambridge, MA, 1985).
8. J. Womack, D. Jones and D. Roos, The *Machine that Changed the World* (London, 1990).
9. See, for example, the texts reporting the IMVP study: K. Clark and T. Fujimoto, *Product Development Performance* (Boston, MA, 1991); J. Krafcik, 'The Triumph of Lean Production', *Sloan Management Review*, Vol. 30 No. 1 (1988); R. Lamming, *Beyond Partnership: Strategies for Lean Supply* (Hemel Hempstead, 1993); and Appendix D in Womack, Jones and Roos, The *Machine that Changed the World*.
10. N. Oliver, R. Delbridge, D. Jones and J. Lowe, 'World Class Manufacturing: Further Evidence in the Lean Production Debate', *British Journal of Management*, Vol. 5 Special Issue (1994), pp. S53-63.
11. K. Williams, C. Haslam and J. Williams, 'The Myth of the Line: Ford's Production of the Model T at Highland Park', *Business History*, Vol. 35 No. 5 (1993), p. 66; K. Williams, C. Haslam, J. Williams, A. Cutler, A. Adcroft and S. Johal, 'Against Lean Production', *Economy and Society*, Vol. 21 No. 3 (1992), pp. 321-53.
12. Williams *et al.*, 'Against Lean Production', p. 352.
13. Ibid., p. 326.
14. R. Overy, *William Morris, Viscount Nuffield* (London, 1976), p. 9.
15. Abernathy, *Productivity Dilemma*.
16. See, for example, Monden, *Toyota*; Ohno, *Toyota*; S. Shingo, *A Study of the Toyota Production System* (Tokyo, 1989).
17. T. Sakiya, *Honda Motor: The Men, the Management, the Machines* (Tokyo, 1984).
18. A. Pilkington, 'Japanese Production Strategies and Competitive Success: Mazda's Quiet Revolution?', *Journal of Far Eastern Business*, Vol. 1 No. 4 (1995), pp. 15-35.

THE MANUFACTURING REVOLUTION

19. A. Harrison, *Just-In-Time Manufacturing in Perspective* (Hemel Hempstead, 1992), p. 79.
20. Clark and Fujimoto, *Product Development*.
21. J. Gardiner, 'Robust and Lean Designs with State of the Art Automotive and Aircraft Examples', in C. Freeman (ed.), *Design, Innovation and Long Cycles in Economic Development* (London, 1986), Ch. 8.
22. Interview with Rover Small Car New Model Centre Manager (PN), Dec. 1992.
23. Cusumano, *Japanese Automobile Industry*.
24. This figure was calculated from the different colour, territory and option combinations available.
25. Harrison, *Just-In-Time Manufacturing*, p.40.
26. Demming developed his principles to guide managers towards building quality organisations; the 14 principles can be identified as one of the major sources of TQM.
27. S. Shingo, *Zero Quality Control: Source Inspection and the Poka-Yoke System* (Stanford, CT, 1986).
28. The term represents both the managers of a process, and the operators who have a great deal to offer in process improvement activities — and should not be excluded in a TQM organisation.
29. For a good description of TQM tools and techniques see N. Logothetis, *Managing for Total Quality: From Demming to Taguchi and SPC* (Hemel Hempstead, 1992).
30. Slack, *Manufacturing Advantage*, p. 40.
31. K. Imai, *Kaizen: The Key to Japan's Competitive Success* (New York, 1986).
32. The economic batch quantity is the number of parts produced which gives the lowest cost for the part when holding and set-up costs are calculated. In JIT the economics are shifted by accounting for the added risks associated with large amounts of stock and the delays and quality problems this can introduce into the production process.
33. S. Shingo, *A Revolution in Manufacturing: The SMED System* (Cambridge, MA, 1985).
34. Lamming, *Beyond Partnership*.
35. S. Nakajima, *Introduction to TPM: Total Productive Maintenance* (Cambridge, MA, 1988).
36. Speed losses result from the operation of machines at inappropriate speeds. The temptation is to run machines at speeds other than the designed running speed in order to synchronise it to the rest of the production line, this causes a high incidence of breakdowns and should be avoided.

3

Collaboration or Collapse?

> *Honda is totally dependent on the North American market ... Late in 1987 it was considering transferring its headquarters from Japan to the United States. This may be good or bad for Britain, and reminds us that the Rover collaboration is small beer to Honda.*[1]

Rover's transformation into a competitive car manufacturer owes much to Honda. In 1980 the struggling BL company had a new chairman, Michael Edwardes, whose strategy for the company's future was based on the introduction of new models. The failed expansion of the BLMC organisation had led the firm into a financial crisis which in turn had severely curtailed investment in new models (see Chapter 1). Edwardes saw the need to renovate and rationalise the company's aging products, but BL was so far behind in the development of a volume-selling, medium-sized family car that the only option open was to buy in a design and manufacture a competitive product under licence. The relationship with Honda was the result; a relationship which has been instrumental in revitalising the fortunes of Rover, not only by giving it access to world-class models and manufacturing technology, but also by serving to introduce new ways of organisation, leading to the increases in efficiency which have put Rover back into profit.

Collaboration has become a common strategy in the car industry. Although it was not immediately obvious what a hugely successful concern like Honda thought it had to gain from association with the struggling Rover company, this chapter sets out to describe just what it was that Rover acquired from Honda and how this knowledge was at the heart of the firm's transformation. The formation of the collaboration itself can be used to gain understanding of other collaborations, both inside and outside the car industry. Many features of the modern business world, such as internationalisation and the transfer of technology, knowledge and systems, and the effectiveness and frequency of mergers and joint ventures, are most prominent in the new structures they have given rise to in the car industry. This subject is much debated; but just how and why the International Joint Venture (IJV) between Rover and Honda came about is not explained by any existing theory on collaboration or the transfer of technology. Instead, it is necessary to examine how the two firms became locked into certain capabilities and strategies by historical developments in the late 1960s and early 1970s.

IJVs are generally seen as attempts to open new markets by companies seeking to spread risks. Porter's model[2] identifies two primary aims: first, to reduce costs incurred in development or manufacture; and, secondly, to gain advantage in new markets or to strengthen a firm's position in existing markets. More recently, however, it has been perceived that a third factor is at work: firms which lack certain desirable capabilities or skills possessed by other firms see IJVs as the cheapest and most effective way of acquiring them.[3] This was certainly Rover's motivation in approaching Honda, and has been a factor in many other IJVs in the car industry. The consequence is that every major international car firm is now involved in at least one IJV (Table 3.1). It is true that these are in part attempts to spread the burden of ever-increasing development costs, and in part a means whereby skills may be acquired. But, most importantly, they represent attempts to discover the secrets of the rise of the Japanese car manufacturers (see Table 1.1).

As Parkhe[4] points out, the literature relating to the strategies and theory of IJVs has reached a difficult stage. A major reason for this stagnation has been a tacit assumption that IJVs represent a complete solution to the strategic problem of how to compete in ever more competitive and narrowing markets with rapidly converging technology and spiralling costs.[5] However, the notion of IJV as a transition stage, as originally proposed by Gomes-Casseres,[6] provides a starting point for fresh empirical discussion of joint ventures which will enable new workable theoretical frameworks to be developed. By describing how one such relationship has prospered, and how it culminated, this study helps make good this omission in current IJV theory.

Table 3.1
Significant Relationships in the International Auto Industry

Company	Own Equity in	Joint Design with	Supply Vehicles to	Supply Components to	Commercial Agreement with
BMW	Rover 80%				
Chrysler	Mitsubishi 12%	Mitsubishi Renault	Mitsubishi (US)	Fiat (Teksid)	Fiat
Fiat		Ford (CVT) PSA, Citroen (MPV)	Nissan, Subaru	Subaru	
Ford	Jaguar 51% Mazda 25%	Mazda (Escort) Nissan (Engine) VW (MPV)	VAG (Autolatina)	KIA Korea Mazda	
GM	Suzuki 5% Daewoo 33% Isuzu 39% Saab 50%	Isuzu (Piazza)	Isuzu (Bedford) Toyota (NUMMI)	Isuzu	
Honda	Rover 20%	Rover		Rover	
Isuzu		GM	GM, Subaru		Chrysler
Mazda	KIA 8%	Ford	KIA	Ford	Saab

Mitsubishi	Hyundai 15%	Chrysler Volvo (MX)	Hyundai Chrysler	Hyundai	Volvo D-Benz
Nissan		Ford	Fiat (SA) VAG (Santana)		
PSA		Renault/Volvo (V6) Citroen, Fiat (MPV)		Rover (R65)	Suzuki
Renault	Volvo 25%	Volvo (Trucks) PSA/Volvo (V6) Chrysler		Volvo Subaru (Engines)	
Rover	Honda UK 20%	Honda	Honda		
Toyota	Daihatsu 15%	Daihatsu	GM (NUMMI)	Daihatsu	
VAG	Seat 50%		Ford-Autolatina Toyota (Hilux)		
Volvo	Renault 20%	Renault/PSA (V6) Mitsubishi (MX)			

Theory, be it of IJV or international management, generally suggests that joint ventures are entered into as positive strategies (see Table 3.2). In Rover's case, however, there was an element of desperation in the adoption of an IJV strategy — arising from the need for an injection of manufacturing and design capability — which placed it on an unequal footing with Honda. The history of Rover prior to the IJV shows how the company, an amalgamation of the rest of the British car industry (see Figure 1.2), had endured a period of declining sales and ever diminishing funds for the development of new models. All this had left the firm with uncompetitive manufacturing facilities and unappealing products. Rover, therefore, had been actively looking to enter a joint venture which would give it access to new markets and new models which it could not have afforded to develop from scratch. The approach from Honda to form a joint venture could not have come at a better time for Rover. However Rover had little bargaining power, and thus the balance of power in the joint venture was more or less like that between a strong parent (Honda) and a weak child (Rover). Neither party in such an uneven relationship invariably benefits in all respects — Rover had more or less to be content with whatever Honda was prepared to give, while Honda in its turn had to be careful not to give away any of its engineering core competencies.[7]

The formation of the Rover-Honda IJV shows from an historical perspective the role that corporate inertia plays in the development of collaborative ventures. Companies can only really benefit if they are clear as to what they intend to get out of the relationship. The conflicting aims of, on the one hand, developing strategies to achieve clear goals, and on the other, of relying heavily on the opportunities presented by past contacts (which may not provide the best partner for the present objectives) are significant to the future development of the auto industry.[8] Are companies going to form into massive global conglomerates, initiated through their IJV interests, or is the industry going to be held back by the inertia present in the existing network of relationships? Examples of both possibilities are evident in the story of Rover and Honda. The short-term benefit which Rover gained from the relationship, namely rapid product renewal, is matched by those gained by its partner: the payment of a licence fee for each unit sold in the EU. However, the reliance on Honda for Rover's new model programme is a serious strategic issue, now that the company has been sold to BMW. Where are the new models capable of maintaining the recovery to come from? The strategic risk has been added to, because although Rover's new partner BMW produces rear-wheel-drive models, Honda provided front-wheel-drive cars; and the continued relationship with Honda is uncertain.[9] At the same time, Honda has, through the joint venture, gained access to European markets and experience of EU competition. This experience will prove invaluable when Honda starts to rack up volume production and sales from its Swindon factory.

Table 3.2
A Taxonomy of Inter-Firm Arrangements

	Non-equity	Equity
Exchange	Short-medium term cash-based contracts	Passive stock holdings Portfolio diversification
Alliance	Mid/long term bilateral contracts (non-cash based)	Joint venture (operating or non-operating), consortium, minority holdings, and cross-holdings
Merger	n/a	Wholly-owned affiliate or subsidiary
Cartel	Price fixing and/or output restricting agreements	Price fixing and/or output restricting agreements

Source: T. Jorde and D. Teece, 'Competition and Cooperation: Striking the Right Balance', *California Management Review*, Vol. 31 No. 3 (1989), p. 31.

The table of collaboration in the auto industry (Table 3.1) reveals several reasons for collaborations among the three major geographical groups of companies: European manufacturers tend to collaborate with other Europeans on cost reduction projects, spreading the funding of new models. Such cases are the joint development of a new large car by Fiat, Lancia and Saab, realised as the Croma, Dedra and 9000 models respectively.[10] This strategy can avoid much of the risk involved in new model development, which typically costs at least £500m and takes three years to complete.[11] The Japanese have striven for multinational status by entering new markets, but the US companies are using global policies of collaboration to protect their future following the weakening of their position in home markets.[12]

Few of these collaborations involve the total commitment of either party, and in consequence few examples have had a major effect on the operating scope of the organisations involved, or radically affect more than one particular market sector or country. GM and Toyota, for example, one of the largest co-operations in production terms, make over 200,000 vehicles a year jointly in a shared facility called NUMMI (New United Motor Manufacturers Inc., California). Yet the number of vehicles produced for GM represents a mere seven per cent of its US sales.[13] The only notable examples of companies having significantly limited their strategic options by deliberately becoming dependent on other manufacturers are Rover and Daihatsu. These organisations have the capability to produce only 50 and 60 per cent respectively of their total sales without having to rely on a major competitor. Daihatsu has declared that it intends to look to the emerging Korean motor industry for more of its material requirements, in order to escape from its reliance on Toyota.[14]

Joint ventures have also been used to gain strategic footholds in relatively inaccessible or risky markets. The joint South African operation of Nissan and Fiat did not affect any other facet of their operations, but enabled them to expand into this previously sensitive market. The creation of Autolatina in Brazil by Ford and Volkswagen-Audi spreads the risk in a relatively poor market. The operation currently makes little profit, but is steadily increasing the influence of these manufacturers in the potentially massive South American market. When collaborations amount to takeovers, that is, when one company acquires a controlling equity stake in the venture, the stronger partner usually has a particular sector of the market in its sights. Ford, for example, plans to take an influential stake in Mazda to develop its small cars. Ford has also acquired Jaguar and Aston Martin, to strengthen its European-derived luxury and sports car ranges. Likewise GM, after fighting Ford for Jaguar, now has interests in Saab and Lotus.

Some collaborations do not fit any of the above categories, and at first glance have no obvious rationale. The troubled involvement of Renault with Volvo, for example, makes little apparent sense, since the two are in direct competition as car manufacturers; but on closer examination the collaboration has the potential to create one of the world's largest and most profitable truck manufacturing groups.[15] The trend in collaborative relationships in the car industry may have slowed from its high level in the early 1980s,[16] but looks likely to pick up again in the late 1990s, as the world economy emerges from a period of slow growth.[17] The total picture of the links between automotive companies is highly complex. Table 3.1 shows only some of the major examples. The complexity is further increased by the takeovers of some of the faltering smaller European organisations which were previously involved with rivals of their new parents, as happened in the case of Rover, at first involved with Honda, now taken over by BMW, and the similar case of Jaguar, GM, and Ford.

There are many other informal, small-scale relationships, the result of a shortage of specialist resources within the industry. This gives rise to the creation of specialist consultation services and test facilities, and the frequent interchange of experts and managers within the industry. An examination of Rover's board of directors shows that most of the company's senior managers have moved from one car manufacturing company to another more than twice in their careers, but collectively have little experience outside the automotive industry (see Table 3.3). The networks of contacts resulting from the interchange of individuals, experts and regulatory bodies are reinforced by historical links — in 1991 Rover Cars was manufacturing body panels for Renault, Rolls Royce and Jaguar because of agreements dating from the 1960s. Jaguar's present owner, Ford, is one of Rover's and BMW's greatest competitors in the UK saloon market.

The automotive industry looks ready for many more collaborations, some larger than any previously seen. There is much speculation that the big US companies — Ford, GM and Chrysler — may be on the verge of alliances.[18] Over-capacity in the European industry may also be leading the smaller members of the European big six to form alliances, in a desperate attempt to cut the costs of introducing their new models.[19] There have been reports of negotiations between Fiat and Peugeot, and also suggestions that Renault may enter an agreement with Toyota or one of the other Jap-

Table 3.3
The Shared Experiences of Rover's Board of Directors: 1994

	Number of Automotive Manufacturing Companies Worked For			Number of Other Industries Experienced during Career		
	1	2	3	0	1	2
Number of Directors	1	8	4	6	5	3

Source: The Rover Group, Corporate Affairs (1994).

anese companies in order to wean itself from its politically sensitive dependence on the French government.[20]

The development of the relationship between Rover and Honda shows the strength of existing contacts in the formation of join venture strategies. After the success of the initial Honda-designed Acclaim there is little evidence to suggest that Rover ever re-examined its position in the relationship. The inertia caused by the deals with Honda, and the familiarity of the negotiating process, led Rover deeper and deeper into reliance on the Japanese firm, a possibility not envisaged according to the international management view of IJVs as strategies to spread risk and enter new markets. Mair states that Rover learnt little from the relationship and quotes a Rover manager as stating that no strategy for learning from Honda existed until 1991.[21]

In order to make clearer just what kind of firm Rover had chosen to collaborate with, it is necessary to consider briefly the history of Honda Motor. Honda is the world's largest producer of motor cycles and started life in the cycle industry. Its founder, Soichiro Honda, like Starley at Rover, made bicycles in his father's workshop before, like Herbert Austin, serving an apprenticeship, in his case, at Art Shokai, a small Tokyo garage. His dream was not to make small cars for the mass market like Austin and Morris, but to build racing vehicles. The link with motor sport has continued since his death. Honda founded a small firm, with the financial backing of family and friends, making piston rings. He managed to acquire a contract with Toyota in 1946. After the war, Honda's interest in engineering led him to experiment on small army-surplus two-stroke engines and in 1949 he developed his own motor cycle. Sales were strong, and Honda joined with Takeo Fujisawa, who not only invested in the firm but brought experience to the sales and marketing operations of the company, allowing Honda to concentrate on the engineering. Honda took full advantage of this freedom, developing a revolutionary four-stroke engine, through which he obtained a big contract with the Katigawa motor cycle company. The success of the engine prompted Honda to stop supplying Katigawa and increase production of his own motor cycles. In 1952 Honda designed a lightweight model, the Cub, which did not appeal to traditional motor cyclists but was a success as a cheap and reliable form of transport. Sales soared; and in 1961 a revised model, the Supercub, reached 100,000 sales.

Honda Motor has consistently behaved differently from the rest of the Japanese motor industry. In 1960, the Japanese government in the shape of the Ministry of International Trade and Industry (MITI) developed a plan to internationalise the Japanese car industry. This plan involved establishing the 'Three Group System', intended to control and encourage the levels of investment in three sectors: mass production cars; mini cars, and special purpose vehicles. By dividing and classifying the existing manufacturers, and limiting the entry of outside organisations into the sectors, it was intended that those firms selected could concentrate on building international competencies rather than worry about competition in the home market. Honda, which after many years of making motor cycles had been planning to start car manufacturing, objected strongly to being excluded, and mounted a protest campaign. The firm gained enough support from the rest of the industry to persuade the MITI to alter its stance.[22] The first Honda car, the S 500 sports car produced in 1962, set the scene for the gradual development of a range of cars (see Table 3.4) whose selling-points were Honda's engineering innovations, including the 1973 Civic — the only car without a catalytic converter to pass the US 1970 Clean Air Act limits on engine emissions.

Table 3.4
Honda Car Production, 1963-92

Year	Car Production	Year	Car Production
1963	136	1978	652,920
1964	5,210	1979	706,375
1965	8,779	1980	845,514
1966	3,209	1981	852,177
1967	87,169	1982	854,463
1968	186,560	1983	857,686
1969	232,704	1984	843,807
1970	276,884	1985	956,410
1971	215,256	1986	1,025,403
1972	235,248	1987	1,021,895
1973	256,962	1988	1,072,773
1974	316,012	1989	1,155,682
1975	328,107	1990	1,223,389
1976	473,597	1991	1,215,054
1977	576,631	1992	1,067,289

Source: Japanese Automobile Manufacturers' Association, *Motor Vehicle Statistics of Japan* (1984 and 1993 editions).

The Honda organisation emphasises the importance of engineers, given the title 'expert' within the company, something which is not unusual in Japanese organisations. However, Honda differs from the normal Japanese approach by having a team of managers to operate the commercial side of the business, separate from but under the guidance of the Honda engineering departments.[23] This reflects the way in which the company was originally organised, when Honda controlled the engineering and Fujisawa the marketing and management. This structure gives the company the flexibility to respond to changes in the market place, whilst also allowing the higher-status engineers to concentrate solely on product design and development.[24]

Sakiya describes how Honda's history falls into four cycles,[25] summarised in Table 3.5. This contradicts a view commonly held within the Rover organisation, that Honda is a company which has progressively pursued growth as part of a long-term, stable strategy, unchanged since the 1950s.[26] Sakiya shows that each cycle, or phase, is prompted by some key event, such as a change in company control, not on an overall corporate design on which the individuals in the organisation have little impact. This view of Honda Motor is supported in the case study by Pascale concerning the 'Honda effect'.[27] This study examined the penetration of Honda into the US motor cycle industry and found, surprisingly, that production of the very successful Supercub was not in fact the firm's original intention. It had originally planned to introduce larger machines to compete head-on against the US and British cycles. However, Honda's employees in the US used the small Supercubs for their own transport and found that these were very popular with the local people. The company seized the opportunity to switch from the larger cycles to the smaller. It would have been unable to do this, had it not developed the ability to switch production rapidly. This flexibility, which allows potential success to become reality, Pascale attributes to the Honda organisation's distinctive management style, and his view is supported by Mair's study of the network of Honda factory operations.[28]

Honda's flexibility is evident in the existence of the three Honda divisions: Engineering, Commercial, and Research and Development, which concentrate respectively on the manufacture, sales, and product development activities of the company. This three-way approach also hinders the growth of factions within the organisation, because each division has its own agenda, quite distinct from the others. In Rover, on the other hand, where distinctions are less clear, different factions in the organisation are constantly demanding alterations to the products to meet their own needs. At Honda, once the original designs are finalised, they do not undergo late alterations. Honda's policy is not to correct any design faults in current models but to ensure that these faults do not occur in future models. Honda's approach to management and the structure of its

Table 3.5
Sakiya's Periodisation of Honda Motor's History

Cycle	Date	Strategy Pursued	Management Style
1	Inception to 1954	Domination of Japanese motor cycle market	Honda and Fujisawa with autocratic control
2	1954 to 1964	Domination of world motor cycle market with the Supercub	Establishment of board and large organisation management style
3	1964 to 1973	Entry into car market with the CVCC engine	Honda and Fujisawa retired, collective leadership style developed
4	1973 to today	International strategy for multinational status	Kawashima's presidency and innovative style

Source: T. Sakiya, *Honda Motor: The Men, the Management, the Machines* (Tokyo, 1984).

organisation is something which has not received as much detailed examination as other Japanese auto manufacturing organisations like Toyota, and is worthy of greater attention.[29]

The company's policy on product differentiation through engineering is sufficiently at variance with those of its competitors to ensure the company's future ability to develop world-class products. This ability should become more and more important as the industry enters a period of over-capacity which is likely to encourage a demand for distinctive vehicles, assuming that the vehicle's costs do not price it out of the market. The factors outlined in this section have shown Honda Motor to be a successful and distinctive organisation, which still has the engineering ability to maintain its position. What, then, did Honda expect when it entered into collaboration with Rover, a failing European motor manufacturer?

The 1970s was a period of great expansion for Honda. Its cars started to sell well in Japan and, like other manufacturers, it needed new markets to keep the expansion going. The first move was into the large North American market, where its compact products and established reputation for motor cycles gave it an advantage over the other Japanese manufacturers, particularly in the Californian market. Honda built a car manufacturing plant in Ohio in 1982 alongside one of its motor cycle factories to serve its growing market share. The success of Honda cars in the USA was due in part to the firm's manufacturing approach, which, as noted earlier, differs from those of other Japanese manufacturers: Honda builds its cars in large batches to a schedule which is fixed six months in advance. In this way, the company believes it can best maintain the engineering standards of the car. It is subtly different from the JIT approach adopted by its main competitors, Toyota and Nissan, which have developed manufacturing systems that respond to customer orders swiftly by manufacturing in so-called batches of one vehicle at a time. As has been shown, Toyota's strategy works very well in Japan, where customers expect to wait a week or so after ordering their cars. But the less patient US customer expects to drive the vehicle away on the spot, and Honda's methods of production and distribution are particularly well suited to meet this requirement. Honda's advantage in the North American market was enhanced, because the JIT approach of its competitors is difficult to implement if parts to be supplied to the factories take more than a few hours to deliver, as is obviously the case with material delivered from Japan. Honda could easily build these extended lead-times into the production schedule, allowing it to concentrate on manufacturing and sales, while its Japanese competitors had the disadvantage of having to concentrate on developing alternative operating strategies to make their JIT systems work.

As Honda was expanding into North America it was also considering Europe. Sales of Japanese cars in Europe had always been restricted by EU import restrictions. Honda had several choices as to how it was to enter the European market: it could take over one of the smaller European firms; it could build an assembly plant as it had in Ohio — the strategy adopted by its competitors Nissan and Toyota; or it could build a manufacturing stake in Europe through collaborating with an existing firm. The first option did not really appeal to Honda. Japanese car manufacturers have been generally disinclined to take over existing plants, since they believe, whether rightly or not, that an established workforce will find it difficult or be reluctant to adjust to Japanese working practices. In the United States, the Japanese firms established their manufacturing plants in rural areas, well away from the heart of the old US motor industry in Detroit. The second option — building a new factory — would probably have been the favoured strategy, but only after the success of the US operation had established a pattern to follow. Mair says that Honda's European strategy was to target German manufacturers such as BMW and Mercedes, instead of the mass-producing big six such as Fiat, Renault, PSA, VW, Ford Europe and GM Europe.[30] And then Rover arrived, looking for a partner. Honda now had a chance to enter Europe immediately, with a strategy which was less risky than trying to build a suitable supply base and transplant factory from scratch.

The start of the relationship between Rover and Honda and its development provide many lessons for strategists and managers. There were five main factors which led to the collaboration: the first, political pressures in the form of EU trade barriers and the UK government's dwindling financial support for Rover; the second, Rover's lack of capital following its record of failure; the third, the lack of design and organisational capability in Rover following the formation and subsequent rationalisation of BL; the fourth, the consumer perceptions of Rover products which demanded a fresh approach to design; and finally, the threat of Japanese manufacturers arriving in the UK market, and forcing Rover to update its manufacturing base.

From BL's point of view, the relationship was intended to revitalise its product ranges quickly and cheaply.[31] This was needed in 1980 because of the rapidly waning enthusiasm of the British government for any further support for the company. Edwardes speculates that if the Metro model had not been an instant success, the cabinet would probably have rejected the scheme to provide £990m out of public funds to support the 1981 and 1982 corporate plans. Edwardes himself managed the collaboration investigation exercise, which involved an analysis of potential partners, and which was undertaken by his own staff, not the existing corporate planning group.[32] The search for potential partners would probably not have begun at this time if the company's relationships with other organisations had not been in the state that they were. If BL had had an existing partner, then that partner would have been the automatic choice for a collaborative deal to provide stop-gap models. During the reformation of the BL board under Edwardes, the idea of associating with Renault had emerged. The possibility had much in its favour, not least the well-structured nature of Renault's operations and its development of advanced models. But Edwardes eventually decided that association with Renault would not be in BL's best interests. He felt that Renault's strongly nationalistic attitude would eventually leave BL no more than a British satellite of a French firm, an assembly organisation restricted to the UK market.[33] GM had also been considered a potential partner. In 1978 Vauxhall's managing director in Britain had approached the BL board with a potential agreement based on the exchange of BL production capacity for GM engineering resources. The plan, called Gemini, was not supported by GM executives in Detroit and collapsed. After these two failures, Edwardes concluded that 'any meaningful collaboration would only be fruitful if the preliminary work was carried through in painstaking detail on a strategic basis. *Ad hoc* ideas were not likely to bear fruit.'[34] It was this which had prompted the dropping of a plan, codenamed 'Dovetail', which entailed the possibility that BL might merge with Chrysler UK, a firm likewise supported by the British Government, and subsequently sold to Peugeot. Again the driving force behind the idea was to acquire the engineering resources desperately needed by BL to develop new models.

In the search for a suitable partner, Edwardes encountered two awkward problems: 'There would be problems within Europe because it is difficult to collaborate with a direct competitor in what is one big market. The dangers of a link with a multinational — even if it were interested — would be that BL would become an offshore assembly operation.'[35] It seemed that if there were to be a solution, it would have to be found in Japan; and Honda soon emerged as the likeliest choice. BL and Honda did at least have something to offer each other, summarised in Table 3.6. Honda had design strengths in just the areas which Rover had allowed to let slip under the BL reorganisations: engines and gearboxes. Rover, for its part, had European design studios, which would improve the styling of the Japanese products and make them more attractive to customers both at home and abroad. Honda's strength of organisation and efficient methods of production, together with the products themselves, were also seen by Edwardes as desirable role models for the new Rover to follow.

Table 3.6
Comparison of Rover and Honda at the Start of the Relationship

Facet of Organisation	Honda	BL
Model range complexity	2	16
Operational complexity, number of plants	2	30
Engineering strengths	Power train	Interior/suspension
Model strengths	Small sector	Executive sector
Other business interests	Motor cycles	Trucks and buses
Management style	Practical/technical	Bureaucratic/historical

Source: Adapted from M. Edwardes, *Back from the Brink* (London, 1983), p. 194, and L. Turner, *Industrial Collaboration with Japan* (London, 1987), p. 55.

The way in which the approach was made towards Honda Motor proved to be a kind of precedent for the future conduct of the relationship. Edwardes enlisted the help of a former colleague from Chloride, who was then the UK's Ambassador in Tokyo, to approach Honda Motor and open negotiations in a formal but humble manner. It took six days for the Honda president to respond to the invitation, showing the great amount of thought that the approach received from the company. This refusal to be hurried into making decisions without due contemplation is characteristic of Honda Motor, but it still surprises and unnerves Rover executives, who are used to having to respond to management requests at only a few hours' notice.

The initial approach was followed a month later by a management meeting on the West Coast of the United States, which resulted in a licence for BL to manufacture a Honda model as the Triumph

Acclaim. Many months passed before the agreement could be finalised. There was a further difficulty, for Honda had set a deadline, requiring production to start within a year, and meeting this was put in doubt by the British government's tardiness in approving the 1980 corporate plan. The final deal left Honda very much the senior partners in the collaboration, and this was not surprising, given Honda's comfortable position and the urgency of BL's needs. Long-term agreements on penalty clauses and the supply of parts favoured Honda; BL had no say in the design of the vehicle; and it had barely enough time to adapt the existing Honda model to fit in with the production facilities available at Cowley. All that was really conceded to BL was its own badges on the car, and some modification to its appearance, so that it at least looked like a BL model.

The Triumph Acclaim project (codenamed Bounty) was followed by several other collaborative ventures. The next project, which was marketed as the Rover 200, involved more collaboration than the Acclaim's manufacture under licence. The Rover 200 was partly designed by BL, but only to make the BL product distinct from the Ballade, Honda's equivalent. The mechanics of the vehicles were largely determined by Honda's engineers. BL's input included the incorporation of one UK-produced power-train unit (the 1600cc engine and gearbox); but the biggest seller, the 1300, was powered by a Honda unit. This project also included a reciprocal agreement for a large batch of vehicles with Honda badges to be manufactured at Longbridge. Unfortunately, the quality of these vehicles was not acceptable. Honda took only a few, and the agreement was terminated early.

The Rover 200/Ballade was followed by an executive car project, codenamed 'XX', and marketed as the Rover 800 and Honda Legend. Again Honda played the greater part in the design, and retained the right to veto all decisions concerning the performance and engineering of the vehicle, further demonstrating the unequal nature of the relationship. The arrangements which saw most of the parts being purchased from Honda continued as in the earlier projects. This was particularly good business for Honda, which supplied the majority of the high value parts, such as gearboxes and most of the engines; only the 2.0 litre engine was manufactured by Rover.

The successor to the 200, the R8 project, was launched as the

Rover 200/400. The initial design was a joint venture, but the derivative Rover and Honda vehicles were tailored by the engineers of the respective firms. The original idea was for the project to be a true joint venture, but it soon became clear that Honda had the upper hand in the negotiations over the design specifications. Rover was left to adapt the design to reflect the new strategy championed by Day for more luxurious vehicles. The R8 agreement included reciprocal manufacturing agreements, with Honda Concerto vehicles being manufactured at Rover's Longbridge plant (see Plate 3.1).[36] This agreement on joint manufacture lasted the length of the project, despite some previous set-backs to this type of deal, such as the rejection of the batch of Longbridge-made Ballade vehicles. Rover was able to expand the range of vehicles during the production life by adding its own updated engines, originally developed for the Rover 800 model. The starting line-up included a 1600cc vehicle with a Honda engine and 1400cc Rover K-series powered cars. These were added to by introducing 2.0 litre and diesel options. Such major changing of designs and model specifications after launching the model is contrary to the usual practice of Japanese firms, which prefer to exert their design energy on the replacement model instead of on extending the short life of an existing model.

The replacement for the Rover 800/Honda Legend was to have been another joint design, but the price was too high for Rover to take part. Rover opted for a face-lift or restyling. It introduced an updated engine, whereas Honda had effectively redesigned the car, keeping it competitive with the offerings from Toyota and Nissan, marketed as Lexus and Infinity respectively. That Honda should pursue this strategy is fully justified by events in the American market at around this time. Honda remained competitive there, but Rover's expensive experiment of selling cars under the Sterling name failed disastrously. Sterlings were over-priced given their level of quality compared to the often cheaper and more reliable competitors from the US and Japan. Rover suffered the same problems of poor customer service which had caused Jaguar to fall into the hands of Ford.

The next joint venture between the two firms was the Rover 600/Honda Accord, code-named Synchro. This model was subjected to a process in which wood panel interiors were styled to match the Rover brand image. The car was available in racing green, but the model

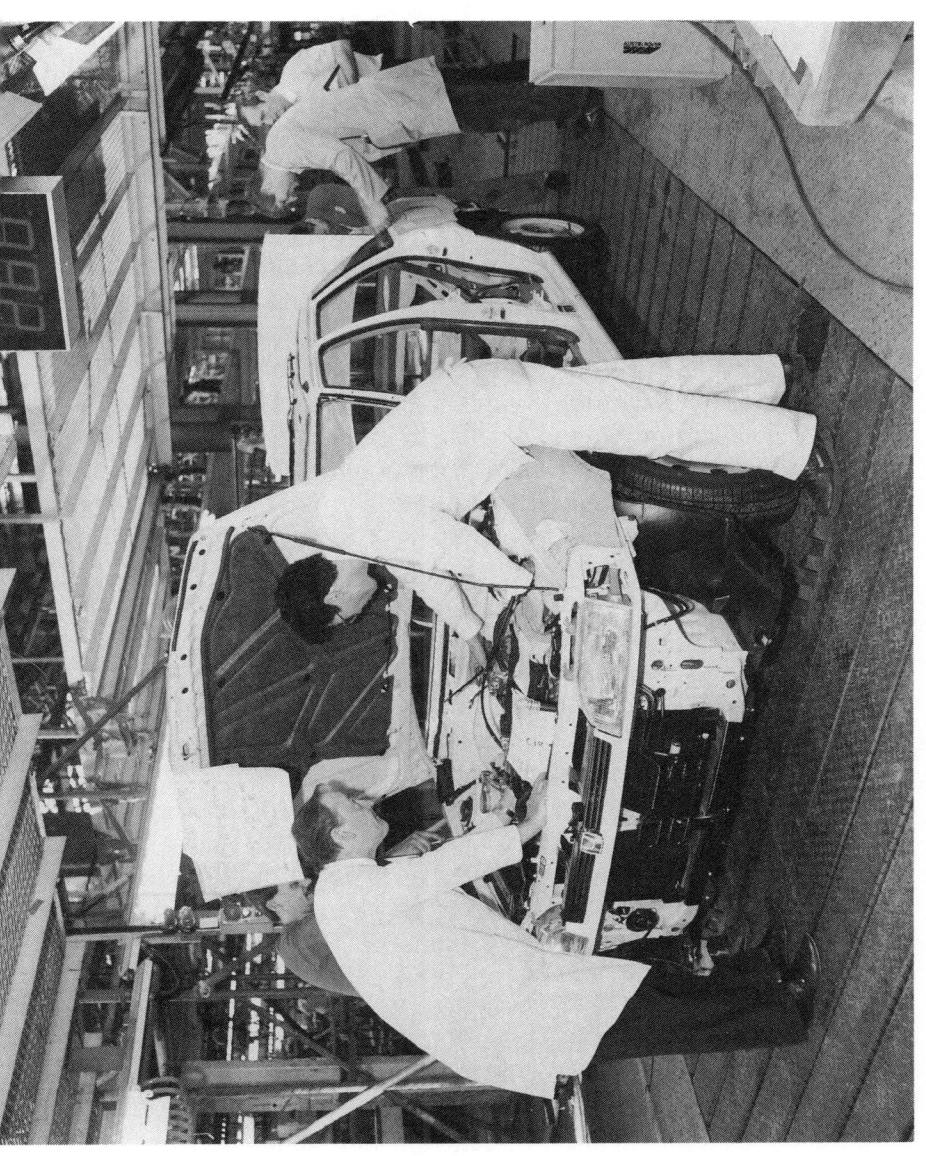

Plate 3.1 Honda and Rover Engineers with a Longbridge-Assembled Honda Concerto, 1990s

was to all intents and purposes a Honda-derived Accord. The Rover 600 contains many Honda parts, the power units initially being mainly produced by Honda. The latest, and probably last, Honda-Rover project was the R8 replacement, codenamed Theta, and sold as the 1995 Rover 400/Honda Civic. This vehicle represents a major facelift for the R8, with updated body-styling and minor alterations to the powertrain, including the introduction of a new diesel. Rover has also introduced its own 1600cc version of the K-series and a 1800cc version which, with hindsight, does protect the company from the consequences of a breakdown in relations with Honda.

The manufacture of panels for the Rover 600 body in Rover's Swindon plant may appear to benefit the British firm. However, as a result of changes in Rover's organisation and accounting practices during the early 1990s, the Swindon Body and Pressings Business Unit is dependent on Honda for 10 per cent of production volume. This is significant when we note that stampings and pressings need to run at high levels of capacity in order so much as to break even, let alone generate surplus cash. Only with the contract from Honda to make the pressings for the Honda Accord could the Swindon plant justify its investment in a modern, fully automatic tri-axis press. Similarly, Honda has increased its level of investment in the UK to further reduce its commitment to Rover, including the opening of a £30m body-pressing centre in Swindon in May 1995.[37] This is part of Honda's recently revealed strategy to offset the strength of the yen by foreign activities, and also to capitalise on the success of the Civic in Europe. The original plan was to build 60,000 Accords and 40,000 Civics in Swindon, but this has been reversed.

The sale of Rover to BAe did not at first disturb the relationship with Honda Motor. The link was in fact strengthened by the equity swap in 1990. This gave Honda Motor a 20 per cent stake in the Rover Group, and Rover likewise 20 per cent of Honda UK with its manufacturing operations in Swindon. The relationship was further strengthened by the added stability and continued relative independence resulting from the sale to BAe. But Honda received a stunning blow when BAe, quite unexpectedly, sold Rover to BMW. The newspaper accounts of the time are full of statements from Honda executives expressing their disbelief that their partner could have treated them so badly. Initial press reports suggesting that Honda would pull out of the joint venture were rather speculative, but had this been the case some 71 per cent of Rover's 1994 Honda-derived output would have been threatened by the run-down of contractual arrangements. Short-term damage to Rover may have been avoided by the salvaging of contracts which were nearly cancelled, when cancellation would have left Rover short of parts or the necessary licences to produce most of its vehicles. But the effect on the rest of British industry and the relationship with Japanese firms could hardly be more damaging. The message sent back to Tokyo was that British firms do not attach much value to relationships built up over many years and are capable, if the situation arises, of turning against their partners with little regard for business ethics.

Current thinking on methods of acquiring new capability often suggests that collaboration can be a highly effective strategy,[38] but there are few case studies to show whether or not this is so.[39] It may at least be observed that once a firm has decided to collaborate with another, it will need in the future to be both flexible and determined, if it is to make the most of the deal.[40] But whatever strength of resolution Rover may have felt at the start of its relationship with Honda was quickly lost as the venture grew and developed, sapped by an unambitious desire for more Honda models. Clearly, this posed a threat to Rover's distinctive identity. The venture was initially a means to acquire a stop-gap product in one market sector until a delayed programme was completed, but Rover has now come to rely on Honda for the majority of its product development activities (see Table 3.7). It has managed to maintain the core skills needed to develop new vehicles, like the Rover 100, but it does not have the financial resources to maintain vehicle development across the full range. An analysis of the current portfolio of Rover products is evidence of its reliance on Honda for design and development programmes: the 800 series is a face-lifted version of the joint development with Honda; the 600 series is nearly identical to the Honda Accord; the 200 and 400 series were developed with Honda as the Concerto and Civic respectively; the Rover 100 was developed from the Metro, the last big independent BL model programme, but had a new engine and a Peugeot gear-box; the Mini was an evolution of the 1960s design made on original production facilities. Rover is caught in a vicious circle in which financial constraints limit the company's ability to design and develop new product fast enough to maintain its range. It generally costs between £1,000 million to

£1,500 million to design and develop a new model from scratch, and it generally takes four to five years to generate sufficient financial resources to fund model replacement. As Rover has made little or no cash surplus for the last 20 years, the rate and extent to which new models can be replaced and redesigned is limited.

Table 3.7
Rover Car Production Split by Platform

	Total Production Units [#]	Production Based on Rover Platform		Production Based on Honda Platform	
		Units	%	Units	%
1981	388,322	367,875	94.7	20,447	5.3
1982	369,839	311,814	84.3	58,025	15.7
1983	433,183	383,141	88.5	50,042	11.5
1984	371,427	339,784	91.5	31,643	8.5
1985	450,892	385,048	85.4	65,844	14.6
1986	389,968	311,231	79.8	78,737	20.2
1987	450,726	313,436	69.5	137,290	30.5
1988	450,575	304,605	67.6	145,970	32.4
1989	434,816	294,831	67.8	139,985	32.2
1990	417,351	229,775	55.1	187,576	44.9
1991	359,951	154,046	42.8	205,905	57.2
1992	339,054	122,400	36.1	216,654	63.9
1993	361,844	122,596	33.9	239,248	66.1

Source: K. Williams, C. Haslam and S. Johal, Who's Responsible? BAe: BMW: Honda: Rover' (unpublished paper, 22 February 1994). [#]excluding Land Rover.

Startling lessons emerge if this situation is compared to that existing when the relationship with Honda first began. Then, Austin Rover had the skills and resources to develop replacement models, but its programmes to replace its ageing models were behind schedule. The deal with Honda was intended to provide a model to produce for two or three years while the Montego/Maestro design was being completed. The situation then was not much different from today's, except for the reputation of the vehicles, which owes much to Honda's engineering. One valuable capability that Rover has learned from Honda is the tailoring of existing designs from other manufacturers to produce 'Roverised' products. This, and the experience in itself of collaboration with another firm, should help the company in its future dealings with BMW. Honda, on the other hand, concentrated on learning about the European market and gaining an understanding of the structure and nature of car manufacturing in Europe. It may not have the same production volume as Nissan has today, but has a greater depth of presence in the supply base.

The Rover-Honda relationship was not a true partnership because it concerned only certain projects covering the development of specific vehicles. The companies maintained a distance between each other, and usually developed separate product plans, with Rover incorporating Honda models into its own plans when these were offered. The injection of Honda-derived models and the resulting programmes has enabled BL to survive as Rover to the present day. The company's reputation for reliability and quality was radically improved by Honda-designed models. Improvements in productivity have also accrued as a result of the relationship, through the adoption and adaptation of Honda's manufacturing facilities and practices, but this has not been without its problems. Adopting the facilities designed by Honda led to several major planning mistakes and false economies, such as the omission of production buffers in the R8 facilities built by Rover, which then had to be introduced retrospectively, to solve production smoothing problems around the engine fitting section of the line. Rover has managed to adopt Honda vehicles and facilities to maintain its survival without completely losing its own identity. Solihull, the home of Land Rover, has been little influenced by Honda, whereas Cowley produces Honda-derived product and little else. The BL-derived culture and values of Cowley were receptive to the manufacturing technology from Honda, but managers there have resisted the product strategy of having large batch volumes and low options for customers, and prefer to move towards an approach closer to that of Toyota. At Longbridge, though, the Austin tradition of mass production of a low variety of cars has enabled the site to become a champion within Rover of the Honda way. It would have been interesting to observe the outcome of the conflict between these two groups, particularly if their different lean production strategies could have been put to the test in the European car market. But this is unlikely to happen now that BMW's plans for the firm as a whole have overtaken events.

Unfortunately, Rover did not learn enough from Honda to solve the problems which led to the collaboration and which probably led BAe to sell the firm to BMW. The original stop-gap measure, intended merely to buy time, acquired a look of permanence, as Rover found it ever easier to relax in its new dependence. The ever greater lack of design capability (both in terms of expertise and resource) was manifest in the management of Rover's limited new model programmes. The company could not support all the models which it would have liked, even with the involvement of Honda. Rover was dependent on Honda for technology and parts for the manufacture of the 800, 600, 200 and 400 models. It could produce the ageing Metro and Mini models independently, but these were relatively unprofitable and did not alone represent a means of securing Rover's future. The Rover 100, a face-lifted version of the previous model updated from the 1981 Metro and incorporating the K-series engine, is the only car produced by Rover which held out any promise of a profitable, independent future. Unfortunately, demand for this vehicle, created by the move away from a cheap and cheerful small car to a sophisticated and slightly up-market vehicle, has not been sufficient to allow the company to match world-class manufacturing efficiency and profit levels, or to move away from Honda for the design of its other products. The opportunity for BAe to sell Rover was a welcome break for the cash-struck defence-based firm.

The effect of the collaboration on Honda, though benign, has been nothing like as great as on Rover. Honda may have been in a position to make a successful takeover bid, having detailed knowledge of the company and its operations, and with Rover having manufacturing facilities designed to produce Honda models, but Honda did not need the extra production capacity, having opened its own plant in Swindon. It is also quite rare for a Japanese company to take over another organisation with which it has established a relationship as a supplier. The smaller organisation is normally preserved intact under a partnership agreement, involving an exchange in equity. This improves the smaller company's operations by injecting capital and benefits the continued operations of both organisations. Honda has gained design expertise in the previously European-led quality and executive cars sectors and also in the particular field of suspension technology. Honda has been able to enter the European market through an indirect route at a time of highly restrictive import controls. The biggest benefit to Honda of the relationship with Rover has been the company's involvement in manufacturing in Europe. This helped Honda to gain gradually previous experience of the labour and marketing practices which it would be operating in Swindon. Its experience of UK manufacturing and suppliers, gained through Rover, places Honda at an advantage compared with other Japanese manufacturers seeking to establish similar operations in Europe. It is doubtful whether the question of the abolition of EC import controls on Japanese cars will alter the strategies adopted by Honda, Nissan and Toyota in establishing manufacturing plants in the UK. These organisations approached the US markets by building greenfield factories managed by local staff, which started assembling Japanese parts but now manufacture vehicles with a native content as high as 80 per cent. A similar approach is likely to be maintained in Europe, so the abolition of import controls is equally likely to remain irrelevant.[41]

What did Rover learn from the collaboration with Honda? The company certainly gained a much needed injection of design capability which has revitalised its image with customers. Its ageing vehicles have been replaced with modern and desirable products that are often compared by the motor press to the established leaders in the field. Rover has been able to produce a full model line-up with input from Honda. The relationship with BMW is less co-ordinated because BMW specialises in rear-wheel drive vehicles. In the late 1980s, BMW did experiment with a front-wheel drive car, but this was soon abandoned. BMW's problem is that it has managed to maintain the 3, 5 and 7 series by incremental adjustments to each model. The question now is whether BMW has the cash resources to maintain a full range of rear- and now front-wheel drive vehicles. Rover will only be able to maintain a design and development function if BMW can afford to maintain funding. Rover has gained an insight into so-called world-class manufacturing techniques and technology, but they not have attained the high levels of efficiency of Toyota's JIT system. However, with the facilities which Rover has in its factories in Oxford and Birmingham, it can build cars at quality levels unheard of in the BL days. Unfortunately the increase in quality has not been matched, despite contrary reports from Rover, with increases in efficiency. As Table 3.8 shows, the level of output from the Rover Group has improved little since the relationship with Honda began, particularly when the decrease in integration of the firm is taken into account. What we observe is the same old BL practice of sacking workers in line with the drop in output, a policy designed simply to maintain productivity levels.

Many Japanese management techniques have been introduced, such as single status canteens, company uniforms and new pay structures, in an attempt to move the responsibility for production performance away from management and on to the shopfloor workers. Some of these techniques may not have had the expected benefits — managers, for example, are still identifiable on the shop floor by the different quality of material in the uniforms they wear — but they have increased the productivity of the factory and cut costs, in line with Rover's European competitors (see Table 8.3). However, these Japanese management techniques have not added up to robust financial performance. Indeed, there has been little change in the financial performance of the Rover company since the joint venture arrangements were first initiated.

The technology which Rover has obtained from Honda has had an uncertain effect on corporate financial and productive performance, and this may have encouraged Rover to be more cautious about the benefits of Honda-derived technology. In particular, Rover did not want to go ahead with V-TEC engine management technology, even though Honda will be using it to develop its engines for the next century. V-TEC limits the opening of one of the inlet valves when the engine is driven gently. This causes the air from the other valve to flow faster, creating the conditions for the engine to operate in lean-burn mode, using less petrol and reducing emissions. When the driver demands it, the engine can perform like a normal unit, providing better acceleration than a normal lean-burn engine. The reduction in emissions means that the car requires a smaller catalytic converter which further increases power and reduces weight. Rover was given only established, well-known engines from Honda, which nonetheless managed to outperform Rover's own and prove less troublesome to customers.[42]

Table 3.8
Productivity Development in BL-Rover, 1955-94

	Sales (units)	Employees (000s)	Crude Cars per Employee
1955	439,600	60,000	7.3
1960	601,400	79,000	7.6
1965	845,600	120,000	7.0
1970	961,700	199,524	4.8
1975	738,200	191,467	3.9
1980	585,000	157,000	3.7
1985	555,500	78,000	7.1
1988	474,687	42,300	11.2
1989	466,619	39,900	11.6
1990	464,612	41,400	11.2
1991	395,624	38,300	10.3
1992	378,797	33,500	11.3
1993	406,804	33,900	12.0
1994	452,500	36,300	12.4

Source: Various *SMMT Year Books*; Company Reports and Accounts.

Rover's separation from Honda may have been foreseen by the executives at BMW, but it cannot be good for the future of the Rover company. BMW does similar design capabilities to those Honda was able to offer, but not the same manufacturing capabilities which Honda passed on to Rover. The question now is whether Rover can develop its facilities independently of Honda to ensure its continued revival, and provide BMW with the insight into Japanese working methods which BMW feels it needs to compete on the international stage. It is even possible that BMW's wish to acquire Rover had little to do with learning Honda's way of business, and much more to do both with overcoming the growing competition in the small executive market, and giving BMW an entry into the rapidly expanding 4x4 market through the purchase of Land Rover. We have already seen in Chapter 1 that the Honda-Rover joint venture did not result in a revival of fortune for the company and that the 'Japanisation' of Rover did not deliver the much vaunted improvements. We must remember that the joint venture was a 20:80 split in which Honda held a minority share of the equity. There was always going to be an air of uncertainty surrounding the relationship. On the one hand, Honda was in a weak situation with regard to controlling the use of technology which was assigned to Rover, and on the other hand, Rover management could not be sure of what product and process technologies would come the company's way.

It was well known that Rover was a weak company that would become increasingly dependent upon Honda for new product and process renewal. Honda, moreover, was a strong parent and could exert its power by denying Rover access to the best product and process technologies available. This behaviour might be expected when Honda did not have a controlling interest in Rover and the future was uncertain. The fundamental problem was that Honda was not locked into full ownership conditions and therefore the obligation to maintain Rover as a viable subsidiary was weakened. The relationship between Rover and Honda was unlike most collaborations in the car industry, in that an atypical imbalance of power existed from the start. The case does, however, provide many lessons for both the car industry and others. The international management literature does not yet fully encompass the ever-increasing number of IJV strategies. The future structure of the world car industry is being put in place by existing collaborations. GM and Toyota's NUMMI (New United Motor Manufacturing Inc.) enables Toyota to build cars in America and GM to see how Toyota makes cars. If it continues, NUMMI could become the basis for one of the biggest manufacturing concerns in the world (see Table 2.1).

IJV theory needs to be developed to incorporate the force driving

Rover: the need to acquire design and organisational capabilities. Collaboration is no longer purely for entry into new markets or spreading risks. Firms increasingly use the strategy in order to learn new techniques and systems of design and manufacturing. These factors can only be identified if an historical view of why the firms entered into collaborative strategies is taken. The theory of joint ventures needs to abandon the notion that collaboration is invariably a positive option for both parties. In most of the relationships in the car industry, one or both parties is being driven by desperation, as was the case with Rover. It is this imbalance which influences the future development of the venture and needs to be considered by both parties, so that they do not lose sight of the original aims of the venture, and avoid ending in a relationship analogous to that of a supplier and drug addict.

Notes

1. S. Wilks, *Industrial Policy and the Motor Industry* (Manchester, 2nd edn. 1988), p. 313.
2. M. Porter, *The Economist Management Report No. 1202*, edited by S. Caulkin (April 1990).
3. G. Hamel and C. Prahalad's papers represent the keys to this debate: 'Strategic Intent', *Harvard Business Review* (May-June 1989), pp. 63-76 and 'The Core Competence of the Corporation', *Harvard Business Review* (May-June 1990), pp. 79-91.
4. A. Parkhe, 'Messy Research, Methodological Predispositions, and Theory Development in International Joint Ventures', *Academy of Management Journal*, Vol. 18 No. 2 (1993), pp. 227-68.
5. M.E. Porter, 'The Competitive Advantage of Nations', *Harvard Business Review* (March 1990), p. 75; K. Ohmae, 'The Global Logic of Strategic Alliances', *Harvard Business Review* (March 1989), p. 151.
6. B. Gomes-Casseres, 'Joint Venture Instability: Is It a Problem?', *Columbia Journal of World Business*, Vol. 22 No. 2 (1987), pp. 7-13.
7. Prahalad and Hamel, 'Core Competence'.
8. This assumes that the auto industry is not disrupted by any other major revelations to disturb the present market and manufacturing structures. The type of disruption I have in mind is the introduction of radical environmental protection policies which would severely restructure the industry.
9. M. Harrison, 'The Rover Takeover: Honda Pours Cold Water on Long-term Relationship', *Independent*, 2 Feb. 1994, p. 2.
10. K. Williams, J. Williams and C. Haslam, *The Breakdown of Austin Rover* (London, 1987), p. 54.
11. J. Glancey, 'Rover 1990', *Independent*, 14 July 1990, p. 27.

12. S. Goldenberg, *International Joint Ventures in Action* (London, 1988), p. 169.
13. L. Turner, *Industrial Collaboration with Japan* (London, 1987), p. 58.
14. N. Cooper, 'Competitive Advantage from Collaboration' (Rover Internal Report as part of a Warwick University M.Sc. thesis, 1990).
15. D. Bowen, 'Renault Merger with Volvo likely in Next Few Days', *The Independent*, 29 Aug. 1993, p. 6.
16. E. Anderson, 'Two Firms, One Frontier: On Assessing Joint Venture Performance', *Sloan Management Review*, Vol. 31 No. 2 (1990), pp. 19-31.
17. K. Harrigan, 'Joint Ventures and Competitive Strategy', *Strategic Management Journal*, Vol. 9 (1988,) pp. 141-58; M. Hergert and D. Morris, 'Trends in International Collaborative Agreements', in F. Contractor and P. Lorange (eds.), *Cooperative Strategies in International Business* (Lexington, MA, 1988); P. O'Brien and M. Tallis, 'Strategic Alliances: The Shifting Boundaries between Collaboration and Competition', *Multinational Business* (Winter, 1989), pp. 10-17.
18. M. Porter, *Economist Management Report*; K. Ohmae, 'Global Logic; The IMVP Study Recorded', in J. Womack, D. Jones and J. Roos, *The Machine that Changed the World* (London, 1990).
19. Goldenberg, *Joint Ventures*, p. 9.
20. *The Sunday Times*, 4 March 1990, p. D7.
21. A. Mair, *Honda's Global Local Corporation* (Basingstoke, 1994), pp. 277-8.
22. T. Sakiya, *Honda Motor: The Men, the Management, the Machines* (Tokyo, 1984), p. 135.
23. Womack, Jones and Roos, *The Machine that Changed the World*, p.169.
24. A. Mair, 'Honda's Global Flexifactory', *International Journal of Production Management*, Vol. 14 No. 3 (1994), pp. 6-23.
25. Sakiya, *Honda Motor*, p. 192.
26. This view is based on the collected interviewing of many Rover managers over a period of four years. See A. Pilkington, 'A Study of Strategy Formulation in an Automotive Manufacturer' (unpublished Ph.D. thesis, University of Aston in Birmingham, 1991) for more details.
27. R.T. Pascale, 'Perspectives on Strategy: The Real Story behind Honda's Success', *California Management Review* (Spring 1984), p. 57.
28. Mair, 'Global Flexifactory'.
29. R.T. Pascale and A.G. Athos, *The Art of Japanese Management* (London, 1981); R.J. Schonberger, *Japanese Manufacturing Techniques* (New York, 1982); M.A. Cusumano, *The Japanese Automobile Industry* (Cambridge, MA, 1985).
30. Mair, *Honda's Corporation*, p. 268.
31. M. Edwardes, *Back from the Brink* (London, 1983), p. 186.
32. Interview with Rover Manager who was part of Edwardes' Central Staff (GS), March 1990.
33. Edwardes, *Back from the Brink*, p. 189.
34. Ibid., p. 191.
35. Ibid., pp. 193-4.
36. Womack, Jones and Roos, *The Machine that Changed the World*, p. 168.
37. A. Griffiths, 'Honda to Speed up £300m UK Investment', *Daily Telegraph*, 10 May 1995.

38. B. Kogut, 'Joint Ventures: Theoretical and Empirical Perspectives', *Strategic Management Review*, Vol. 9 (1988), pp. 319-22 discusses this opinion in terms of transaction costs; J. Kay, *Foundations of Corporate Success* (Oxford, 1993) describes it as an organisational strategy.
39. J.M. Geringer and L. Hebert, 'Measuring Performance of International Joint Ventures', *Journal of International Business Studies* (1991), pp. 249-63 have tried to analyse the success of the joint venture itself but there appears to be little emphasis on the success for the companies involved.
40. Y. Doz, 'Learning through Manufacturing Alliances', in P. Dempsey (ed.), *Manufacturing Europe 1992* (London, 1991); Hamel, 'Core Competence', p. 80.
41. Mair, 'Honda's Global Flexifactory'.
42. Interview with Rover Manufacturing Manager (GB), Sept..1992.

4

Keeping the Options Open: Warwick University

The Advanced Technology Centre is just one aspect of the strengthening partnership between Rover Group and the University of Warwick. The need to develop people to manage the technologies of the future has been the spur to bringing together an ambitious programme to enhance the skills of Rover's managers and engineers. The University has provided a lifeblood of engineering talent for Rover Group. More than 300 Warwick-trained people have gone on to take up employment with Rover and a further 600 Rover people have been trained on jointly-developed university courses at Warwick.[1]

We have observed in the previous chapter that the relationship between Rover and Honda was subject to a high degree of uncertainty in which trust could not be taken for granted. In an earlier period the Rover Group had entered into external collaboration with Warwick University, in order to produce a joint programme of training and development in the field of new technologies. The relationship with Warwick was maintained throughout the joint venture with Honda. We do not wish to represent the Rover-Warwick relationship as a strategic alliance similar in nature to the Honda-Rover partnership, but to make the observation that Rover was keeping its options open. The relationship with Warwick University centred on two key individuals who wanted Rover to maintain a degree of independent capability which could possibly, in time, lead to the rebirth of the business. Similar steps intended to strengthen the core activities of the firm were also taken by Rover's board of directors, who enlisted the help of several management consultants with a view to diluting the firm's dependency on Honda, whilst retaining the benefits bestowed by the link. The arrival of the tide of consultants at Rover is discussed in the next chapter; this one describes the Warwick effect.

Most of the UK's older universities were established in the nineteenth century with a great deal of help from wealthy benefactors, many of them industrialists. In receiving this help, they were incidental beneficiaries of class sentiment; for they were conceived in the spirit of the advancement of learning and the preservation of civilised values. Men who were interested in producing literate and numerate workers would set up technical colleges, not universities; and there is little doubt that much nineteenth-century cash came from relatively uneducated people who admired, but did not understand, universities. This one-sided relationship could not last. Industry itself became more intellectually self-confident with the obvious increase in complexity of both the technology of manufacture and the techniques of management. Industry needed more recruits of graduate quality; universities were moved to supply them, with a consequent shift from the arts and pure sciences to applied science, practical psychology, and more recently, business and management studies.

At present, the financial constraints on higher education have greatly encouraged universities to seek collaboration with industry; and it is likewise in the best interests of industry to do its best to ensure that universities in this country continue to be centres of technological excellence.[2] But as long ago as 1970, it had become clear (as reported by the CBI-Vice Chancellors' Committee on Industry, Science and the Universities — the Docksey Report)[3] that collaboration between industry and the universities was not only desirable, but was actually taking place. The Docksey Report suggested that much of the contact between the two was a matter of chance; an unforeseen encounter at a conference or other function might lead to positive, or at least quantifiable results; it might equally lead nowhere. The importance of these contacts in helping to produce successful partnerships has been stressed in several reports and their value has never been disputed. There is still much debate as to how these contacts can be encouraged, but there appears to be a consensus that they must be handled carefully from the outset, because how they begin may well affect the whole of the future relationship.[4]

It has been argued, particularly in the UK, that government involvement is the most effective way of generating these personal links.[5] However, evidence gathered by the OECD tends to show that governments can do little of value in this area, since 'intimate and effective relations have seemingly owed little or nothing to governmental initiatives.'[6] But there would hardly be a greater number of these contacts in the absence of governmental initiatives. Personal contacts are fairly difficult to reconstruct in a study of university-industry collaboration. These relationships, successful or unfruitful, are not documented, and the original links become obscured by any subsequent co-operation. The formal relationship normally receives maximum publicity from the leaders of both organisations involved (whether or not they themselves were instrumental in forming the relationship) and any other third party involved, such as national and local government, which may provide grants. In a study of 200 Scottish academics, Connor found that 'the most frequent forms of contact arose through formal and informal visiting and through requests for advice and information'.[7] Connor analysed the origins of personal contacts and concluded that the link was slightly more likely to be the result of an approach from the industrial side. Saunders, by contrast, found that the initiatives were predominantly derived from the academic sector, rather than in response to industry-based requests.[8] This is explained as a result of the need for universities to be 'actively marketed' to encourage industry to increase their proportion of external research funding.[9] One surprising finding of Connor's survey was the unwillingness of academics to divulge their contacts to colleagues; 'it was suggested by respondents that recommending others, whose capabilities were perhaps unknown, could perhaps jeopardise the continuing credibility of existing relationships.'[10] This clearly limits the proliferation of personal contacts, particularly in fields where access to research case material or technical support is rare.

The value of training in industry and how it should be managed is a much debated subject, but few people doubt that it should be a key part of any industrial country's strategy for improving its international standing. In the UK, there has been a move in recent years to the involvement of industrial organisations, through Training and Enterprise Councils (TECs) and the like, in helping to design the courses offered by education establishments. The development and teaching of co-operative courses, arise normally from consultations between existing contacts, or third party initiatives. Collaboration over course development has received much publicity lately. Both industry and academia are agreed on the need to offer courses which train and educate present and future employees. This is best achieved by first establishing industry needs, then tailoring the courses accordingly. It has been encouraged by many training boards and government schemes: 'engineering departments are now being positively encouraged to collaborate with industry to make sure that the courses they provide are relevant to the needs of industry.'[11] One of the largest contributions by a third party has been made by professional institutions, such as the Institute of Mechanical Engineers. For clarity, courses can be categorised as those for undergraduates and those designed for post-experience education. The term post-experience education covers postgraduate, non-research higher degrees and diplomas, and short course training initiatives offered by organisations through the involvement of higher education institutes.

Co-operation in the UK at the undergraduate level, particularly in the technical areas, has primarily developed from recommendations contained in the Finniston Report of 1978-79, which considered the future of the country's engineering skills. The Report recommended a change in traditional engineering courses and advocated the introduction of broad-based courses like the new B.Eng. and M.Eng. degrees.[12] The Finniston Report also recommended an increase in the number of sandwich courses: 'periods of industrial-professional training are planned to integrate with the periods of academic study in a pattern appropriate to the particular discipline'.[13] Only three years after Finniston, there were 16,000 of these courses. The increase in them is desirable, provided that the placement part of the course is well managed and not used as a means of helping to fund students through periods of unemployment. The benefit of a sandwich approach (either thick or thin, depending on the length and number of industrial placements) to the student is that it gives direct experience of the working environment and its practices. Possibly the biggest benefit of these courses is that the liaison between academic and industrial supervisors feeds back into future course material. 'Engineering educators must themselves be aware of the needs of industry, of modern design and problem solving techniques, of industrial processes and of the financing and management of engineering. Industrial liaison is of paramount importance at every stage of the development of a course, and through its execution'[14] and, since the supervisors work with industrial contacts, 'it also leads to a better understanding between university and the employer and often to a practical co-operation in research and development work.'[15]

A consultative approach to course development is not uncommon in the rest of the world, and there are some examples of a far greater extent of co-operation. Siemens, the electronics firm, selects the students for an undergraduate course at the Technical Universities of Munich and Berlin. It is not rare for entire classes to be recruited from the course and into the company. Philips and Eindhoven University have a similar relationship, though this entails more than purely course development and is examined later. The General Motors Institute (GMI) in Michigan, an independent but closely coupled 'co-operative education' college, was formed in response to approaches by GM. The realisation by the local authorities that the collapse of the U.S. motor giant would mean the devastation of employment prospects in the city of Flint encouraged GMI to be set up as a joint venture to ensure that a high calibre workforce was available for the GM plants.[16] GM now has a stake in the venture, which is now known as the GMI Engineering and Management Institute.

An increased provision of tailor-made undergraduate courses may help colleges by easing the task of recruitment, with classes being provided by the industrial organisation on the understanding that courses will include industry-specific subject matter. The demands of the industrial partner may therefore restrict the training given. The providers of courses should be careful not to lose, as part of their aims, the development of the students' intellectual capabilities. The development of intellect may be discouraged by a more vocational bias and over-dependence on one source of income — or one outplacement body. Nevertheless, the importance of relevant training, provided by industry but divorced from academic involvement, may be seen in an international example, Japan, where there has only recently been any co-operation between universities and industry. 'In Japan, college industry co-operation has been regarded as taboo since the 1960s when the student movement was at its most active.'[17] This forced the development of internal educational processes at all levels within Japanese industry and encouraged firms to concentrate specifically on their own educational needs, leaving colleges to concentrate on developing academic and intellectual strengths. The success of the Japanese as an industrial force may be partially attributable to this segregation of academic and vocational professional education, because both branches can aim for excellence in their own sphere.

The level of co-operation in post-experience education is normally higher than that in undergraduate training, with post-experience education courses being tailored for individual companies or small groups of companies. The courses often involve case studies and working examples derived from the industrial organisation, and are jointly developed with a large input from the collaborating company. The courses normally lead to masters' degrees, M.Sc. or M.B.A., or diplomas, and rely on the industrial organisation to release managers and executives to take part. Most larger, progressive companies offer such chances to their executives, and this level of involvement is fairly widespread. Short courses are also widespread. Most concentrate either on new developments, or on refreshing areas of skill and knowledge which may have been last studied by the employee over 30 years ago. These courses are normally instigated by professional institutions or university staff. Short courses may also be the result of in-house initiatives. Land Rover, for instance, offered a series of lectures examining new technology with Birmingham Polytechnic, which sought to promote the understanding of advanced manufacturing technology (AMT) in the company.

One of the primary objectives of the academic community is to extend the boundaries of knowledge through research. The involvement of industry in research has been limited in the past, because of the dedication of academic institutions to pure research, rather than its applications. For though the external industrial funding of research has long been recognised as potentially very helpful to universities as a whole,[18] it is not welcomed by all academics, some of whom prefer that the ultimate aim of their studies should remain the increase of human understanding, and that their work should not be distorted into providing practical applications for industry. Furthermore, much research would not attract funding from central resources, particularly under current trends. Industrial support would be needed, for example, for market studies and non-mainstream manufacturing technology with only limited practical use.

Several means of developing and administrating industrially supported research in higher education establishments now exist. They can be classified using Stankiewicz's framework: liaison offices and officers, consultancy companies, and university-industry consortia.[19] Liaison offices have proliferated during the 1980s. Every old university and polytechnic sector university now has at least a contact point for industrial enquiries, and many have an entire technology transfer department, compared with only 15 such institutions at the time of the Docksey Report. The function of liaison units vary, but it is normal for such units to present to industry the available expertise, to co-ordinate university resources and to provide the legal and contractual management necessary in the undertaking. These are important skills which university staff have never needed to acquire in the past. Their provision from a central point ensures that the commercial integrity of the contracts and intellectual property rights are maintained.

Consultancy companies were defined by Stankiewicz as 'university affiliated quasi-commercial organisations which sell the consultancy services of academic scientists affiliated with them.'[20] These consultancy companies may, on the surface, resemble the liaison offices of certain universities. There is, however, one important difference between them. The companies are in direct competition with other external consultancy firms. The Docksey Report envisaged this state of affairs, and warned that the universities would have to be careful not to be seen to undercut the regular consultancies by off-setting their consultation costs against teaching and other centrally funded activities. They were thought able to do this by combining consultancy work with their already subsidised research activities. This fear appears groundless, since most academics successfully divorce their teaching and research activities from the contracted consultancy, and many follow the reverse process by using consultancy income to subsidise research.

University-industry consortia are special examples of consultancy companies which may often be supported by more that one organisation. Their success has largely been in the utilisation of advances in electronics and computing. Because of the resources required to support such a centre, these have primarily been limited to the USA, where multinational companies use them in a pooling of expertise and funding. The advantages of consortia over other types of initiatives are due to the scale which can be achieved. Some of the research projects are just too big for individual universities and companies to support. For smaller projects, the consultancy and contract approaches are more suitable. Consultancy companies can provide total solutions, including a high degree of project management, but are not as adept at developing links and technology transfer as the more traditional liaison-office-based research projects, because they are based on a formal relationship, rather than on informal contact with a view to solving a particular problem.

Research as an educational activity — Ph.D. and M.Phil. degrees — enjoys the advantage of attracting central funding in the UK from the various research councils. Schemes like co-operative awards in science and engineering (CASE), industrial studentships and Total Technology, all aim to make traditional university-based research available to industry, and to bring to the academic world experience of industrial practice.[21] They can reduce a company's research costs. They also have a broad base, tending to encourage a balance of different disciplines in order to arrive at a compromise solution to a genuine problem of industry: 'the Total Technology Scheme provides Ph.D. training by means of problem-solving projects in, and of importance to, companies or other collaborating bodies. Each project requires research study and course work which crosses boundaries between academic disciplines.'[22]

The future of research sponsored by industry looks certain, but the methods of generating contracts will probably radically change in the near future. The OECD report suggested that 'if the universities ever had this liaison function to themselves, they no longer do so, now and in the future it is likely that the pressure of competition will drive the universities into trying to identify as yet unoccupied market niches.'[23] The researcher concludes from his own experiences that such research should be encouraged, not only because of the shared financial burden and application of academic research to industrial situations, but also because it offers a unique multidisciplinary training for future industrial managers to develop their intellectual capabilities.

The UK-based Teaching Company Scheme began in 1976 as a joint venture between the Science and Engineering Research Council (SERC) and Department of Industry, now the Department of Trade and Industry. Its main aims are to encourage the development of new technology in industry and to promote interaction between university and industry. 'The scheme involves commitment by a firm and a university to tackle a programme of work in the firm.'[24] It is not uncommon for more than one firm to be involved in a particular teaching company. The Land Rover-Jaguar-Birmingham University Teaching Company, 1986 to 1989, was concerned with introducing new manufacturing technologies, such as robotics and laser welding. A teaching company is jointly managed by senior staff from the university and co-operating company or companies, with an external consultant appointed by the SERC.[25] The teaching company, if successful, may lead to further co-operation and other teaching companies examining different problem areas. Success appears to depend on the accurate and realistic management of the programme, and consistency in the mutual expectations of the partners involved. 'The primary advantage to the industrial partner is the access to specialist knowledge and techniques and through this an unprecedented opportunity for industrial experiment and low risk evaluation of innovation processes. The industrial environment provides a practical 'test bed' for existing research and may formulate new research areas.'[26] The change and training processes attached to teaching companies may not end with the cessation of the scheme, because often the associates (personnel employed in the teaching company) are retained within the company and so 'take the knowledge gained from the university with them, that is real technology transfer by people transfer.'[27] The benefits of teaching companies in the cross-barrier flow of ideas are great, but because the relationship is very formal, it may not lead to any closer long term co-operation or integration between universities and industry. The scheme between Land Rover, Jaguar and Birmingham University, for example, was not extended despite its success and the subsequent employment by the companies of 50 per cent of the associates. The prospects of continuing or reestablishing the teaching company were not helped by the divisions which developed between the commercial organisations when Jaguar was privatised and subsequently left the Rover Group. Neither organisation could afford to fund a replacement teaching company alone.

The idea of the science park was developed in the United States after the war. The principal motivations have been the increased profitability of the universities through real estate activities and the nurturing of a high technology industry sector. 'The idea is to create in the vicinity of universities, sufficient room for small high technology companies and the R & D laboratories of larger ones. It is hoped that this will lead to the development of dense networks of informal contacts, consultancies and joint projects between the host universities and the companies in the parks.'[28] Different science parks are set up for different reasons and with different intentions. Most, but not all, exclude mass production activities, some exclude established companies, whilst others aim at attracting the research laboratories of multinationals. The funding of the parks is also very varied, which leads to different types of tenant organisations. The funding is nearly always from the public sector, either through the university itself or from local and national government.[29] There are approximately 35 science parks in the UK, 100 in the rest of the EU, and almost 100 in the USA. However, their success is hard to gauge. Stankiewicz argued that the success of these ventures could not be measured, since most are too new, and should only be judged according to the long-term profitability of the companies they nurture. The Docksey Report and the OECD study of university-industry relations both determined that there were more company failures than successes in the science parks. This supports the belief that the conditions required for successful parks are not fully understood.

An advantage of science parks as against other university-industry ventures is that researchers exploit their own innovations. This means that the parks avoid such difficulties as confidentiality, mismatched needs, patent right difficulties and conflicts over industrial and academic values and attitudes. Furthermore, the risk of failure is effectively exported to a private company, which may sink or swim, so that any failures do not reflect on the university or industry. There is some evidence that the success rate of start-up companies in science parks is higher than outside,[30] but this is by no means conclusive. One of the most successful parks, apart from Stanford, Route 128 in Boston and the Research Triangle Park in North Carolina in the USA, has been the UK's Cambridge Science Park (CSP). Established in 1973, the CSP was the result of the Mott Report[31] being taken to heart by Trinity College. The CSP and its effect on local industry has been examined in some detail.[32] But though it appeared to be successful in the 1980s, this was largely due to factors beyond its control, which in that area have historically led to the creation of successful high-technology firms such as Pye, Acorn and Sinclair Computers. The CSP report states that it accounts for 'a little over 10 per cent of the high technology scene.'[33] Recent reports have suggested that CSP companies have been hard hit by the recent decline in economic growth.[34] As part of the university-industry collaboration mechanism, the contribution of the science parks has been small in comparison to their rapid growth. This is possibly because of the very strong emphasis on commercial exploitation rather than partnership. The future of the science park concept seems assured, but it is not a primary means of integrating industry into the academic environment. It is rather a means of generating capital for universities.

The establishment of independent research institutes creates a classic university-industry interface. Institutes normally have close relationships with local universities, and are concerned with a particular area of research and the training of professionals within that field. There is a risk that an institute's specialisation may limit its potential market, but this seems to vary from industry to industry and country to country. Institutes are available for contract research, which because of their focus on industrial rather than academic study, reduces the problems that secrecy and ownership rights can cause by hindering other forms of co-operation. The most prolific institutes established in the UK are those supported by the Wolfson Foundation. These cover many areas of applied research: semiconductors at Birmingham, acoustics and vibration at Southampton, heat treatment at Aston, metallurgy at Imperial, off-shore engineering at Heriot-Watt, and several others.

An international example is SINTEF (the Foundation for Scientific and Industrial Research at the Norwegian Institute of Technology) in Norway, which is closely linked with Trondheim Technical University. This model of institute operation has been copied by the University of Linkoping, in Sweden and the Pulp and Paper Research Institute of Canada (PAPRICAN) at McGill University. The Dutch government has set up three regional microelectronics centres in Delft, Twente and Eindhoven which are closely related to the local technical universities. These centres provide services to the industry which is concentrated in these areas, much along the same lines as the Edinburgh-based Wolfson Institutes of Microelectronics and Applied Computing furnish Silicon Glen (the area of high technology development in Scotland). It is important for institutes to maintain strong links with universities, for without this they 'will "degenerate" to the same status as private contract research laboratories or the "branch laboratories" of industrial associations'[35] and lose contact with the advances being made in the academic world.

The next step in increased co-operation between universities and industry is a positive joining together of the organisations involved. This partnership may be exclusive of any other organisation or, as is most likely, involve only certain departments within each parent organisation, leaving the remainder to form and develop their own contacts if they wish. The partnership stage may be extended into full merger or union which should, because of the depth of the relationship, exclude the possibility of significant collaborations with other organisations. There are presently no true examples of this, the closest being Eindhoven University and Philips. Because of the employment structure of the town, the two have grown together and depend on each other, Philips on the university for provision of qualified and skilled employees and basic research, and the university on Philips for much of its funding. Other examples are more apparent than real, since the universities have normally been created by large industrial concerns and have had no previous independent existence. Interestingly, an example of this type of institution, GMI in Michigan, has recently moved away from total dedication to GM and now contracts training and research from other organisations. It is this partnership stage that the Rover-Warwick relationship has reached. Beyond partnership, at the merged level of co-operation, each organisation theoretically loses its own corporate identity, so that there is no longer a true collaboration. If a university or one of its departments becomes so close to a particular organisation, it is in a much better position to influence that organisation, but may lose its standing as a credible academic entity. This may limit the quality of staff and students which it is able to attract and prevent the company from gaining any more capability than it already has from the partnership arrangement.

The most evident product of the relationship between Rover and Warwick is a jointly funded and staffed research centre at Warwick called the Advanced Technology Centre (ATC). The development of the relationship is shown in Figure 4.1. The association of Rover with Warwick University is based on the rapport between Professor Kumar Bhattacharyya of the Manufacturing Systems Engineering Group at the University and Andy Barr, Manufacturing Director,

Rover Group until November 1990. In the earliest stages of the relationship in the mid-1970s, Bhattacharyya was part of the Production Engineering Department of Birmingham University and was involved in undergraduate projects. Through various projects and student placements, regular contact was made with Bill Horton at Sherpa Vans in Washwood Heath, Birmingham, which led to a teaching company to examine the suitability of an inventory management system in light truck manufacturing, based on personal computers.

The teaching company was successful and led to the formation of four more teaching companies in co-operation with Birmingham University. Their fields included simulation, low pressure sand casting and abrasive belt machining. The involvement of the BL board and manufacturing managers in the early stages of these projects brought about the first contact between Bhattacharyya and Barr,[36] whose authorisation was needed for Rover's funding of the projects. Barr and Bhattacharyya established a close relationship which still remains today, as a result of their concern for manufacturing technology, and their similar characters, both having forthright natures. In 1980 Bhattacharyya moved to Warwick University to take the chair as Professor of Manufacturing Systems Engineering.[37] The importance of this move was very significant for the subsequent development of the relationship, since Warwick allowed Bhattacharyya greater freedom in his involvement in Austin Rover. The problems Austin Rover had at this time were 'highly visible, needing short term reward but also the need to develop for the future.'[38] Bhattacharyya thought that the process required to provide these rewards and long term prosperity was hindered by the organisation's existing structure; 'no matter what strategy you had you couldn't implement it ... the majority of the directors were barons, fiefdoms ... most of the people in the organisation were survivors and highly political, we needed to inject new people to overcome this.'[39]

The personal relationship which had developed between Bhattacharyya and Barr was strengthened with the joint development of a recovery strategy for Rover.[40] This was formalised at Rover as the Integrated Technology Strategy (ITS) of 1980. The ITS aimed to use technology to achieve flexibility in Rover's manufacturing operations and so alleviate some of the organisation's pressing busi-

Figure 4.1
The Development of the Relationship between Rover and Warwick University

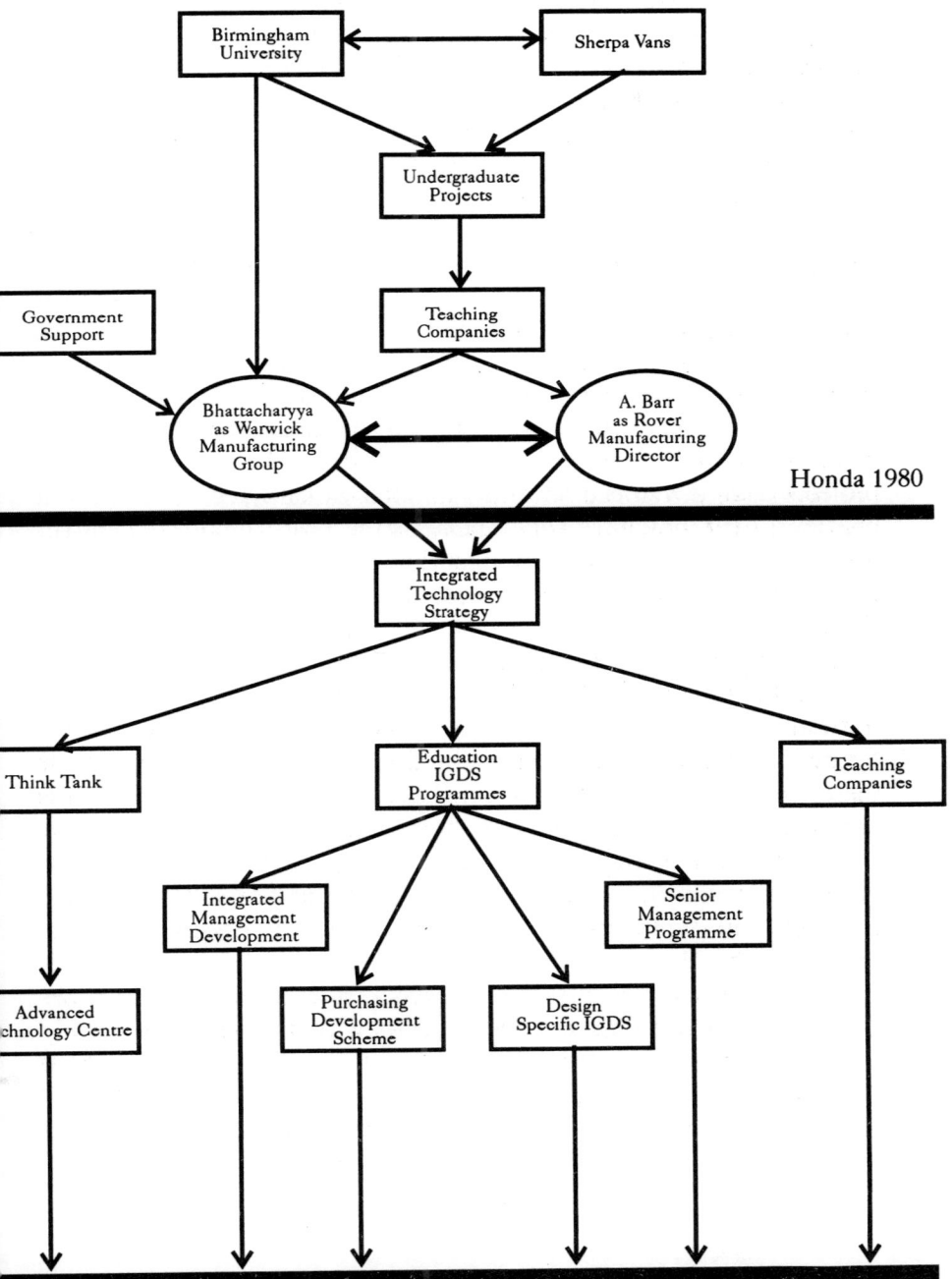

ness problems; a 'manufacturing [rather than product or marketing] led recovery was necessary.'[41] The strategy also involved expanding technological training in the organisation, or 'investing in people', as the strategy termed it. The increased training was provided by initiatives like the IGDS (Integrated Graduate Development Scheme)[42] and a large teaching company. The ITS assumed that any model development for the near future would be a joint operation with Honda, and that Austin Rover's input would be limited because of the company's weak financial position; but the new model would provide time for gathering strength to break out into the international market.

The teaching company developed from the ITS has grown, and is now one of the largest and longest running in the country. It has been largely involved with the introduction of new techniques and facilities across Rover's sites, and specialises in production and material flow simulation exercises. Strangely, the reputation of the manufacturing technology activities developed by the teaching company is not high amongst Rover's manufacturing departments. Teaching company projects have developed several solutions which have created more problems than they have solved. One is the FMS (flexible manufacturing system) in the Longbridge Power Train Business Unit; another, the R8 (Rover 200/400 model) line-balancing performed by the simulation team.

The IGDS (Integrated Graduate Development Scheme) originated, at the same time as the ITS, from a government initiative to examine the value of M.Sc. degrees to industry. This initiative was taken up by the MSE Group with help from previously established contacts with Rover and consultations with BAe and Lucas. The scheme was later widened to take in entrants from other organisations and now boasts 50 such participating companies. The IGDS scheme was created to introduce advanced manufacturing technology and techniques to managers. The scheme still has its original modular structure, with each student attending fourteen modules over a two-year period, normally on a week's block release. The students are assessed on coursework completed in their own time and normally involving the application of module material to a work-related problem. There is also a final dissertation on an area of relevance to the student's own work. The IGDS was extended in 1989 to cover design activities as well as the manufacturing disciplines. The IGDS is a unique example of co-operation in postgraduate training between university and industry, where the industrial organisations not only provide students and funding but are also deeply involved in the course management and teaching. Case study material from co-operating companies and discussions with senior managers are also common in the modules. Industrial supervisors are appointed to assist each student through the course. One concern about these types of courses is their incestuous nature — young engineers from a company attend courses presented by their own managers, using case studies from their own firms.

Another course, the Integrated Purchasing Development Programme (IPDP), intends to widen the view of the company's buyers, and enable them to see their activities in the context of the company as a whole, rather than in the narrow context of price reduction alone. Senior managers are also trained through specially tailored courses and IGDS modules, as part of the collaboration between Warwick and Rover. A recent development was a D.Eng. (Doctor of Engineering) degree, an M.Sc. with an extended research project, which is reported to go beyond the level of a traditional Ph.D. in four part-time years. The compression of such detailed and intensive work into so short a time is truly remarkable, particularly given that the first year's intake included senior managers in the company, including the manufacturing director, who had not undertaken any formal study for many years.

An ambition of Rover's last chairman before the sale to BMW was to be able to offer everyone in the company the chance to partake in any education or training activity they chose, irrespective of the relevance to their work.[43] This has been realised by the creation of the Rover Employees Assisted Learning (REAL) scheme, by Rover Learning Business (RLB), introduced in 1991. The REAL scheme entitled any employee to a £100 annual bursary for part-time study outside normal working hours. The firm has also taken the operations of Warwick's MSE Group as a basis for introducing many NVQ qualifications, based on the work experience of its employees with little external assessment.

The relationship between Bhattacharyya and Barr after the ITS led to the introduction of cell managers. This is a production management technique which involves the setting up of small work units (called cells) on the shop floor with a mini-managing director (the cell manager) in control of nearly all the functions connected with production from the cell. This technique is now widely applied across the company and is likely to be extended to give the cell manager even more control and autonomy. The relationship between Barr and Bhattacharyya has also led to the adoption of several JIT principles under the title minimal inventory control (MIC). However, MIC brought about JIT delivery of material from warehouses to the trackside for batch building, rather than true JIT manufacturing, as at plants operated by Japanese firms. The effect of MIC has been to move the stocks in the firm from the factory and suppliers into distribution centres, but not to reduce them. The company's performance on stock turnover has shown an improvement, when compared to the mid-1980s and the arrival of Honda, but only to the levels seen in the 1950s, and this should be viewed in the light of decreased integration (see Table 4.1).

Table 4.1
Changes in Rover's Stock Turnover Rates, 1955-94

Year	Stock Value (£m)	Sales (£m)	Stock Turns (%)
1955	38	221	5.8
1960	55	311	5.6
1965	85	526	6.1
1970	322	1,021	3.1
1975	531	1,868	3.5
1980	946	2,877	3.0
1985	789	3,415	4.3
1993	745	3,831	5.1
1994	854	4,477	5.2

Source: Various Annual Reports and Accounts.

The arrangement between Bhattacharyya and Barr for generating ideas was formalised in late 1984 into a 'think tank', which included other executives from both groups (Rover and MSEG). It is in this forum that the idea of the ATC was developed. The 'think tank' has since become the ATC Steering Committee. The stated purposes of the ATC for Rover are 'to create an environment, in purpose-built premises, where a mix of Rover staff and university staff could work together and share facilities. This pooling of skills and experience has created a focus, not just on technologies at the leading edge of automotive manufacture and development, but also in the development of people.'[44] In summary, these are first the transfer of knowledge and skills into the company, and secondly the creation of an environment away from the daily business to allow a clear vision of the future of the company. This section is intended to outline the nature and future potential operation of the ATC part of the Warwick-Rover relationship. The ATC has been promoted as a centre for strategy development, being removed (though not too distantly) from the daily environment of production and the pressures for results which this exerts. The work of the ATC is outlined in the table of projects (see Table 4.2), but essentially covers technology application and a small amount of manufacturing-based policy and planning work.

The centre was built by the university and rented to Rover and Rolls Royce (Aero Engines). The Warwick manufacturing group uses the University's procedures to enable its staff to become involved in the centre's projects without formal releases, and provides Rover personnel with access to equipment, but has monopolised the relationship by preventing other departments from the University, including the highly regarded Business School, from becoming involved. The other tenant of the building, Rolls Royce, has a stronger link with the manufacturing group than with Rover, but its link with the University is not nearly as far developed as Rover's. The Rolls Royce part of the ATC is concerned with materials research, particularly in the area of advanced ceramics. It has little of the mixing of staff intended in the Rover-Warwick relationship, possibly because Rolls Royce's management of the relationship takes into account the firm's extensive research capabilities elsewhere.

As to the ATC's future, it has always been stated that personnel will be encouraged to use the centre as a transition point, where skills can be developed and then redeployed back into the organisation's operations. The centre's position in the development

Table 4.2
The Work of Rover's ATC Groups, 1992

> Manufacturing Policy Unit
> IT Strategy Group
> Vehicle Thermodynamics
> Intelligent CAD
> Advanced Chassis Design
> Adaptive Engine Management
> BOM (Bill of Materials)
> Vehicle Electronics Development and Testing
> Catalytic Converter Development
> Expert Systems Application
> Facility Simulation
> Thermal Imaging
> Suspension Control Development
> Electronic Interface Testing
> Injection Moulding
> Advanced Assembly Techniques

Source: Warwick University, *Advanced Technology Centre Brochure* (1992).

of technological advances in both product design and manufacturing techniques is well defined, and it is here that the co-operative nature of the relationship is presently most fruitful. This side of the centre's operations are under the direct control of the ATC steering committee, which consisted, until November 1990, of Barr, Bhattacharyya, the engineering, manufacturing and planning directors of the company, and two senior lecturers from the university. The intended people strategy role of the ATC is less to the fore than declared in the ITS or in other public statements of intent. There is no fast turnaround of staff back into the operational areas of the company. There is, however, an increasing trend towards involving senior and middle managers in specific project discussions and management groups based there. The ATC does have certain advantages for Rover employees working there. It has a pleasant location, being withdrawn from production pressures. Its location on the university campus has enabled Rover personnel, through the use of the university's library facilities, to conduct wider searches of information than are available through the company's own resources; and it enables some managers to develop their own personal understanding of technological and management issues, and as a base for their own independent studies for higher degrees.

Another large Midlands-based company with long-established links to a university is Lucas, the electrical and automotive suppliers. It is helpful to contrast the relationship between Lucas and Birmingham University with that of Rover and Warwick. Between the wars, the Lucas board had recognised the value of highly qualified people to their organisation, and practised a selection procedure which examined graduates from Cambridge, Leeds, Manchester and Birmingham Universities.[45] The process also involved developing two-year training courses within the company, with the intention of producing better engineering or production managers than were available through the traditional methods of recruitment and training, 'Taking a wider view, the Lucas directors decided that they would be doing a service to the industrial community of Birmingham in general and to themselves in particular, if they provided the money for the University of Birmingham to set up a postgraduate department of production engineering.'[46] This was started in 1944 but was slow to develop, reportedly due to the University's desire to use the funds provided to research a particular engineering area, rather than on education in the fields of production and management.

The department was relocated in 1953 from prefabricated buildings to a large house near the university and became the Lucas Institute of Engineering Production. But another 20 years passed before the institute was provided with proper facilities, again solely funded by the company. The failure of the university to help in developing the relationship distanced the Institute further from the University. Internal differences within Lucas also reduced the influence of this relationship. Several senior Lucas people preferred to work with staff at Birmingham College of Advanced Technology (later to become Aston University), because of the 'practical atmosphere of the Aston College of Technology [whereas] the Birmingham University people tended to live in an ivory tower.'[47] Yet the relationship with Aston did not flourish either, probably because of the lack of formal support from the Lucas organisation as a whole. The latest Lucas Professor of Manufacturing Systems Engineering, John Parnaby, has had great influence on the company, but not as a result of co-operation with the University. Parnaby worked full-time for Lucas as Managing Director of Lucas Engineering Systems[48] and promoted the introduction across almost all the company's manufacturing activities of the simple removal of non-value-added activity.[49] This strategy improves the efficiency of an organisation by reducing wasted effort, transport, material and so forth. The relationship between Lucas and Birmingham University now consists of the contracting of certain limited research activities to the University through the company's research centre, which has replaced the Lucas Institute. The informal links with the University still exist, but have not been developed on a co-operative basis.

The move from Birmingham to Warwick by Bhattacharyya had a major, and influential, effect on the relationship's ability to prosper. This is illustrated by Lucas's continued, and eventually failed relationship with Birmingham, whilst Rover's relationship with Warwick has flourished. The history of Warwick University makes its operation very different to that of Birmingham. Warwick was founded in the 1960s as part of the government's plan to increase the availability of locally-supported higher education. The opportunity to support the new university was taken by Warwickshire County Council, Coventry City Council, Lanchester (Coventry) Polytechnic and local industrialists (among them Lord Rootes, William Lyons and Gilbert Hunt). There were many debates and arguments over control of the new university and its charter. The controlling influence was finally gained by the industrialists, who created an organisation which functions in a way unlike most other universities, specifically 'the Vice-Chancellor's style of operation, [as reviewed in] the Tyzack Report, the apparent attempt to limit democratic processes and to ensure the loyalty of administrators and staff, the peculiarly subordinate relationship with 'industry' — and the degree of power exerted by a few industrialists on the University's Council — all these may indicate a situation in Warwick which is, in some ways, unique.'[50]

The continued involvement of industrialists since the University's turbulent days in the 1960s, when student demonstrators uncovered conspiracies in the University Council against certain staff and students, has led to power being concentrated in the Council and its industrial advisers. There are also few restricting regulations which would prevent the establishment of a venture like the ATC. A similar move by a single professor to enter into a collaborative venture of the size of the ATC would be almost impossible in the pluralistic world of most university senates, where it would be insisted that the relationship should benefit the whole academic community and not just part of it, as occurred at Birmingham with the Lucas investment. The Warwick organisation actively fosters independent entrepreneurial activities and has supported the MSEG's movements towards providing the training requirements of Rover and Rolls Royce.

Honda was only ever weakly involved in the Warwick-Rover collaboration in which an ongoing relationship generated the design and manufacturing elements in the ATC projects. Whatever else, the Warwick-Rover arrangement confirms that the Rover was interested in maintaining some independence when ATC type projects could have been given to Honda. Warwick was being used by Rover as a backup which reduced its dependency on Honda. The use of Warwick in this way has never been publicly declared, but is borne out by Barr's expressed fear that Honda was not providing Rover with the most appropriate technology, and was restricting its future options.[51]

The ITS is still reflected in the firm's manufacturing strategies — the need to rejuvenate the manufacturing capabilities of the firm in isolation from any product- or marketing-led recovery which other parts of the organisation may be pursuing. However, the technology which resulted from the relationship has not been a resounding success. The managers and shopfloor personnel in the firm have been acclimatised to some elements of AMT (Advanced Manufacturing Technology), but have had to invest much of their own time and resources to get the turn-key solutions working effectively. Many Rover personnel have been through the training courses and M.Sc. programmes at Warwick, which will have prepared them to form visions and strategies for the firm, but may not have provided the technical and intellectual stimulus that other courses could have offered, particularly as a result of the closed nature of the course teaching and assessment processes. A major influence on Rover arising from the Warwick link has been the ATC. The building itself gives Rover managers a chance to remove themselves from the daily pressures of their jobs and concentrate on strategic issues. The staff recruited by the Manufacturing Group to work in the ATC have been useful catalysts for the many project teams which circulate through the building, without having a major role in the firm itself.

The departure of Barr to a BAe firm saw a decrease in the significance of the relationship to Rover, with an effective cessation of the high level discussions between Bhattacharyya and Barr (the MSEG did develop similar projects with the BAe subsidiary firm which Barr went to run). The emphasis in the relationship is now on the new manufacturing organisation in Rover: Product Supply. Without Barr at the helm the relationship could have floundered, but the arrival as manufacturing director of Alan Curtis, one of the relationship's biggest supporters, looks to have secured at least a reduced role for the near future, at least until the impact of BMW becomes clear.

Notes

1. 'Rover and Warwick University: A Close and Developing Partnership', Rover Press Release on the Opening of the Advanced Technology Centre by Mrs Thatcher, 8 Jan. 1990.
2. Third Report from the Select Committee on Science and Technology, *University-Industry Relations* (1976), s5.10.
3. *Industry, Science and Universities: Report of a Working Party on Universities and Industrial Research to the Universities and Industry Joint Committee (the CBI-Vice Chancellors' Committee)* (London, 1970), known as the Docksey Report.
4. R.M. Rosenzweig with B. Turlington, *The Research Universities and their Patrons* (Berkeley, CA, 1982), p. 43.
5. B. Crossland, 'The Life-long Education and Training of Mechanical Engineers', George Stephenson Lecture, *Proceedings of the Institute of Mechanical Engineers*, Vol. 200 (1988), p. 143.
6. OECD, *Industry and University: New Form of Co-operation and Communication* (Paris, 1984), p. 20.
7. A.I.Connor, 'College/Industrial Liaison: A Survey of Academic Perceptions', in *Positive Partnerships: Papers Presented at 4th World Conference on Cooperative Education, Napier College* (Edinburgh, 1985), p. 416.
8. J. Saunders, 'Profit through Partnership', in ibid., p. 380.
9. OECD, *Industry and University*, p. 48.
10. Connor, 'College/Industrial Liaison', p. 416.
11. Crossland, 'Life-long Education', p. 143.
12. M. Finniston, *Engineering our Future* (London, 1980), Section 4.18.
13. Committee of Vice Chancellors, *Universities and Industry* (London, 1981), p. 13.

14. G. Brown, 'The Need for University/Industry Collaboration in the Development of Engineering Education', in *Positive Partnerships*, p. 188.
15. Committee of Vice Chancellors, *Universities and Industry*, p. 13.
16. W. Cottingham, 'Closely Coupled Cooperative Education', in *Positive Partnerships*.
17. 'Academe, Industry relax Ivy Walls to Cooperate', *DTI Overseas Technology News* (London, April 1988).
18. Finniston, *Engineering*, Section 4.18; Third Report of the Select Committee on Science and Technology, Section 5.10.
19. R. Stankiewicz, *Academics and Entrepreneurs: Developing University-Industry Relations* (London, 1986).
20. Ibid., p. 53.
21. C. Wood and R. Leonard, 'The Design and Implementation of a Flexible, University-Wide, Total Technology Programme', *Proceedings of the Institute of Mechanical Engineers*, Vol. 6 No. 4 (1978), p. 289.
22. A.J. Cochran, 'Interdisciplinary Higher Degrees Scheme', *1987/88 Aston University Annual Report* (Birmingham 1988), p. 96.
23. OECD, *Industry and University*, p. 49.
24. Committee of Vice Chancellors, *Universities and Industry*, p. 15.
25. W.M. Kilkenny, 'The Teaching Company Scheme: A Construction Industry Case History', in *Positive Partnerships*, p. 454.
26. Ibid., p. 456.
27. P. Davies, 'Integrating Universities and Companies' (Warwick University Seminar Paper, Nov. 1986), p. 8.
28. Stankiewicz, *Academics and Entrepreneurs*, p. 55.
29. UKSPA (UK Science Park Association), *Science Parks and the Growth of Technology Based Enterprises* (London, 1987), p. iii.
30. Ibid., p. 31.
31. 'The Relationship between the University and Science Based Industry', *Cambridge University Reporter* (Cambridge, 22 Oct. 1969).
32. Segal Quince & Partners, *The Cambridge Phenomenon* (London, 1985).
33. Ibid., p. 41.
34. Interview with Cambridge accountant, Dec. 1990.
35. Stankiewicz, *Academics and Entrepreneurs*, p. 60.
36. Interview with ATC Director (PD), Oct. 1989.
37. K. Bhattacharyya, ATC Opening Speech, 9 Jan. 1990.
38. Interview with Bhattacharyya, Feb. 1990.
39. Ibid.
40. A. Smith, 'The High-Tech Teacher who's Setting the Pace', *The Sunday Times*, 6 March 1988.
41. Interview with Bhattacharyya, Oct. 1989.
42. A. Lorenz, 'Rover Drives Toward Niche — Honda-Style', *The Sunday Times*, 8 Oct. 1989, p. D8.
43. Interview with Rover Chairman, G. Day, March 1990.
44. Rover Press Release, 'Rover's Advanced Technology Centre Exploring the Frontiers', 8 Jan. 1990.
45. H. Nockolds, *Lucas: The First Hundred Years* (London, 1978), p. 112.

46. Ibid., p. 112.
47. Ibid., p. 113.
48. J. Parnaby, 'The Design of Competitive Manufacturing Systems' *International Journal Technology Management*, Vol. 1 No. 3/4, p. 385 (1986).
49. J. Parnaby, 'Creating a Competitive Manufacturing Strategy', *Production Engineer* (July/Aug. 1988), p. 24.
50. E.P. Thompson, *Warwick University Ltd.* (London, 1970), p. 16.
51. Interview with Barr, Oct. 1990.

5

An Impossible Leap?

> *It's a sobering thought that no one employed by a car company has to buy a car from a dealer (they buy in-house through the company instead, or even receive a free car as part of their compensation package). Thus, they have no direct link to either the buying experience or the customer.*[1]

In Chapter 4 we noted that Rover Group management pursued policies which kept the company's options open. As an integral part of forging the relationship with Honda and striving towards changing management practices, Rover's management enlisted the help of external consultants. Their job was to create the conditions of panic which would then engender support for the politics and process of change deemed to be required. We shall review the various stages of this process, starting with the earlier Breakthrough policy and ending with benchmarking studies. The common denominator of all of these approaches was the assumption that, by changing organisation practices, world-class performance could be obtained.

The firm's central strategic planners were developing policies which, they argued, could build on the lift to the business which Honda would give. We have already demonstrated in Chapter 3 that the Honda-led recovery was more promise than actuality, but this was not always seen to be the case. In the late 1980s, most senior managers believed that Rover's fortunes would be reversed and, if the company could properly exploit the relationship with Honda, it would emerge from its difficulties in good health. In order to justify that which was already decided, the company called in US management consultants to help Rover re-think its strategies. One such approach was Breakthrough. Breakthrough is an approach to strategy implementation and organisational change developed by various management consultants. The idea of Breakthrough is to generate a 'step change', a rapid and major improvement in an organisation's activities which elevate it to a higher level of competitive advantage which incremental change alone cannot achieve.

The business environment is set to become increasingly competitive. Many theories concerning the creation of profitable firms have been developed. Most are characterised by a belief that a radical change in a company's operations is normally required for it to survive and prosper. These theories have been supported by many examples of how top companies achieve success. In particular it has been noted that a coherent transition theory must have elements of capability assessment, context specifity and the identification of change as a process. A straightforward reconstruction of events is not enough. Table 5.1 shows some exponents of what can be termed 'company turnaround' theory along with the emphasis of each approach. One major difference between the change methodologies shown in the table is in the degree of change prescribed. Breakthrough is an application designed to alter the operations and culture of the organisation permanently. Stopford and Baden-Fuller, whose work examined six manufacturers in mature industries which have managed to generate and sustain profitable growth,[2] termed this type of change 'rejuvenation' because of its impact on organisation activity rather than just on a company's operations.

Table 5.1
Existing Literature Concerning Organisational Renewal

Name	Type	Focus
Cosby[3]	Turnaround	Quality
Deming[4]	Turnaround	Quality
Drucker[5]	Turnaround	Management
Goldratt[6]	Turnaround	Logistics
Grinyer[7]	Turnaround	Management
Hayes/Wheelwright[8]	Rejuvenation	Organisation
Imai[9]	Rejuvenation	Organisation
Juran[10]	Rejuvenation	Quality

Kanter[11]	Rejuvenation	Planning
Kay[12]	Rejuvenation	Organisation
Mather[13]	Turnaround	Logistics
Ohmae[14]	Turnaround	Organisation
Ohno[15]	Turnaround	Logistics
Pascale[16]	Rejuvenation	Organisation
Peters[17]	Rejuvenation	Organisation
Porter[18]	Rejuvenation	Planning
Schonberger[19]	Turnaround	Operations
Shingo[20]	Turnaround	Manufacture
Skinner[21]	Turnaround	Manufacture
Wight/Plossl[22]	Turnaround	Logistics

The difference between turnaround and the other form of renewal generation, rejuvenation, is perhaps best described with reference to a review of Peters' original 43 excellent companies which were used in the popular book *In Search of Excellence*[23] and reviewed by Pascale.[24] The survey found that only 14 of Peters' 'excellents' remained in the top 500 in 1987, only five years after the original study. The failing companies were examples of turnaround, not rejuvenation. The companies which have maintained their success may be examples of rejuvenations, or just the result of extended turnarounds. In summary, rejuvenation should put a firm in a position to adapt to any future crisis, whereas a turnaround organisation would normally fail in a crisis.

Rover adopted the Breakthrough approach towards the end of 1989 following the appointment of a new Managing Director, George Simpson. Breakthrough involves generating changes which should produce a company which is world-class in all its operations (note the similarity to Mintzberg's structural configurations, they being an attempt to establish how organisations can achieve 'getting it all together').[25] The underlying belief is that over time firms begin to suffer from restricted vision, an almost routine, unconscious acceptance in their operations of limitations which are effectively self-imposed, and not necessary. These limitations, or barriers, are termed 'paradigms' or 'mindsets'. Breakthrough believes that these barriers can be surmounted if they can be clearly identified and addressed — the destruction of a mindset-barrier is known as a 'Breakthrough' and significantly improves the organisation's performance. The methodology adopted in Breakthrough ignores all the usual mental barriers in the organisation's self-perception, and establishes multidisciplinary teams, each concerned with addressing one of a set of corporate goals. These goals are derived from a vision of what the organisation needs to do in the future to become an outstanding firm in its field.

In essence, Breakthrough involves the establishment by the company's leaders of new aims of an hitherto unconsidered kind, and the generation of strategic plans for achieving them. The rejuvenation starts when the organisation is striving for these Breakthroughs — the act of developing radical and challenging strategies introduces a culture in which the organisation is continually challenging itself to improve its performance. In many ways it is similar to the Japanese continuous improvement approach, *kaizen*, which is hardly surprising, given the source of the idea. Breakthrough was developed by various US consultants, and was derived from the work of Pascale at Stanford University on Japanese management.[26] The idea was then taken up by a group called Transformational Technology Inc., a concern offering executive training courses for use by independent management consultancy firms.[27] The network of consultants around Transformational Technology Inc. encouraged the idea of Breakthrough to spread. The operation of the network is varied, as shown by the fact that, in their Breakthrough initiatives, Rover and the UK-based oil company BP used different firms of consultants. But the use of different consultancy firms also shows that much the same idea can be transmitted through different channels.

In 1988 Schaffer expounded the virtue of what he termed 'Breakthrough Strategy'.[28] This should not be confused with Pascale's Breakthrough as it differs from it in some respects. But in its guiding principals, Schaffer's method is essentially similar to Pascale's approach: 'The Breakthrough Strategy advises managers to by-pass all the preparations and excuses and to get going directly, at once, toward a short term result, a success',[29] but uses an incremental methodology to achieve the Breakthrough which is much closer to the *kaizen* method described by Imai.[30] Schaffer's Breakthrough is based on developing an atmosphere within the organisation which encourages all its employees to make rapid but small advances towards the company's future goal. It intends, if the correct culture has been established, that these small Breakthroughs should add up to a large step change. This is another example of the rejuvenation concept, but is intended to be achieved in a fundamentally incremental rather than revolutionary manner.[31] Schaffer argues that a Breakthrough surge becomes necessary because 'it's hard to see below the surface because defensive behaviours mesh with management practices, organisation habits and company policies and procedures, forming barriers that inhibit, scatter, and dissipate the corporate resources'.[32] Schaffer identifies several fundamental built-in barriers to organisation success which need to be attacked to create a rejuvenation. These barriers include: psychological tunnel-vision, wasteful management patterns, low expectations, misuse of work management disciplines and 'invisible conspiracy: the underside of corporate culture'.[33] Schaffer advocates a top-down cascade training method, where the messages are passed through the hierarchy in a series of briefings, as the best means of educating the organisation about Breakthrough.[34] Much of Schaffer's text explains how to manage this cascade exercise and how the critical activity of goal setting should be carried out.

The principal differences between the approaches of Pascale and Schaffer can be seen from the development by Miller and Friesen[35] of Mintzberg's work on organisation structure configurations.[36] Miller and Friesen's study revealed the existence of a small number of very common configurations and observed that 'if organisations changed in a piecemeal and disjointed way, altering elements of strategy and structure quite loosely and independently, they would constantly be realigning their profiles, moving from one state to a randomly different one.'[37] If changes are not subject to an overall plan, and to the control of the organisation as a whole, the process of constructive change does not get properly under way; this will eventually lead to difficulties requiring much more drastic and sudden changes, which might have unforseen effects on the nature of the firm. Pascale proposes that removing mindsets is the way to creating rejuvenated organisations, though he prefers the term 'excellent'. Hence much of

Pascale's Breakthrough methodology deals with the analysis of mindsets or management paradigms and working out how to change them. It is this prospect which the management consultancy firms offer to prospective client organisations.

Breakthrough came to Rover at the request of, and under the control of, the Managing Director, George Simpson, and closely followed his appointment in January 1989. This appointment was a result of the sale of Rover to BAe by the Government and followed the elevation of the previous MD, Graham Day, to the position of Rover Group Chairman. Breakthrough followed approaches to Rover by the US consultancy firm Charles Smith and Associates. The idea of utilising consultants was unlikely to have occurred to Rover's previous leadership. Day believed that there was no need for them: any expertise required by Rover should have been available within the organisation itself, given its size and its rich legacy from the British automotive industry: 'everything Rover need to do can be achieved through evolution'.[38] Day was quite adamant that Rover should not attempt a step change because he doubted the ability of the organisation to cope with complexity. The arrival of Simpson as managing director was a crucial factor in the adoption of Breakthrough in Rover. For although Day had no time for consultants, Simpson, being new to the post with all its responsibilities, was more receptive. When the consultants approached him, he would have been trying to work out his own aims and strategies for the Rover Group. The development of Breakthrough within Rover is shown in Table 5.2.

The first stage was the selling of Breakthrough to Rover's CEO by the consultants, and entailed a review of the company's operations and objectives. This attempt to establish a clear purpose was undertaken with the help of the then Strategic Planning Director, Roland Bertodo, who had previously been advocating a radical overhaul for the firm.[39] Another significant factor which induced Simpson to accept Breakthrough was that at this time Rover was experiencing financial and operating difficulties, despite the profits generated by the restructuring in the run-up towards the company's privatisation. The promise of quantum improvements in performance and prosperity held out by Breakthrough had a very strong appeal. From a consultant's review of the company's activities, Simpson developed, with the support of the Strategic Planning Department, a list of aspirations which he wanted the company to achieve: first-class customer service, world-class quality and world-class productivity. These aspirations were to be used to direct the company's Breakthrough initiative and are not entirely surprising, since they set out a desirable position for any company. But aspirations are of little use without strategies for achieving them; they have to be more closely defined, so that the firm can be clear as to precisely what, in measurable terms, it has to do. The managing director's office, therefore, set to work on comparative studies, provided by the Strategic Planning Department, of Rover's competitors in the UK, and finally decided that, for the turnaround to be a success, the following requirements had to be met: a 30 per cent reduction in operating costs; first place in the Customer Service Index (CSI, the National Car Buyers Survey index of customer service quality); 50 per cent of sales to be exports; 80 per cent of customers and dealers to see Rover as service standard bearer; and 6 per cent return on sales.

Table 5.2
The Adoption of Breakthrough at Rover

1	New MD takes charge at Rover
2	Consultants gain conviction of Rover MD
3	Development of the Breakthrough aims
4	Main Breakthrough projects
5	Sub-projects
6	Implementation issues crossing organisational
7	Loss of support

The process of arriving at these figures illustrates one particular problem facing a firm which has fallen behind the competition. The aims which are decided upon are calculated from what is best practice at the time of calculation, and not what will be, when the plans have been put into effect two or three years hence. In two or three years' time, for example, what satisfies today's customer will appear obsolete or be uncompetitive. This is particularly true at present, when the UK car market is set to become greatly affected by the new manufacturing operations of Honda in Swindon, Toyota in Burnaston, Derby, and Nissan in Washington, on Tyneside. If this has happened by the time that Rover has achieved its aims, it is likely that the company will still be well behind the major manufacturers in the industry, who will have made significant improvements on their present performance. The value of such comparative benchmarks is discussed at some length by Hamel and Prahalad, who wisely believe that 'imitation may be the sincerest form of flattery, but it will not lead to competitive realization. Strategies based on imitation are transparent to competitors who have already mastered them. Moreover, successful competitors rarely stand still'.[40]

Hamel and Prahalad's exposition of what constitutes effective strategic thinking concludes that all successful organisations, Western and Japanese, share a company vision to which the whole corporate machinery is directed. Hamel and Prahalad call this vision *strategic intent*. They state that it should encompass more than just an image of a significant improvement in the organisation's operations; it should also include an active perception that the organisation will continually change, and continually redefine its aims in order to become rejuvenated. The development of such an active management paradigm is one of the fundamental aims of the Breakthrough approach. Hamel and Prahalad go on to suggest that Rover should not have been so ambitious as to take the market leaders as models for comparison. 'The lesson is clear: assessing the current tactical advantages of known competitors will not help you understand the resolution, stamina, and inventiveness of potential competitors.'[41] Rover is a small firm in comparison to other automotive manufacturers, yet it still believes itself to be a major player in the industry, and persists in setting itself the unrealistic aim of being as good as the market leaders and different from them. The truth is, however, that these leaders are in a different market and operate with fundamentally different constraints. Rover's persistence with this inappropriate vision is probably the legacy of the Ryder era at British Leyland, when the company was still a global player.

Once the aims of Breakthrough were established, a number of brief executive conferences were held, to work out the implications of the measures for the operations of the company. From this discussion, no fewer than 14 projects emerged — the Breakthrough Projects, each being led by a director and each with a loosely defined area within which to achieve the improvements which Simpson demanded. As ever when projects are loosely defined, it is not often possible to keep sight of what the overall policy should be, and many managers could use the project to justify strategies and policies which they had always wanted to implement, rather than work towards developing a coherent set of policies, congruent with the new Breakthrough strategy which Simpson was hoping for. Some of the projects, such as those aimed at radically lifting the level of overseas sales, failed to see beyond the normal ways of working and faltered. But the Breakthrough approach did manage to improve other operations. It increased, for example, the efficiency of distribution by changing the allocation of finished vehicle stocks. The existing system involved sending all the finished vehicle stocks into the dealer networks, where Rover was unable to manage them effectively. With the new method, Rover holds the stocks centrally, and can therefore rapidly distribute the vehicles ordered by customers, rather than having to transfer cars from one dealer to another, to the benefit of neither. The new system has also improved the efficiency of manufacturing activities by concentrating regular production on the top-selling variants, leaving the others to be dealt with as special orders for which customers have to wait. The production schedules are now much more predictable, allowing Honda's manufacturing systems to work in the way that they were originally intended.

British Petroleum (BP) also embarked on a Breakthrough programme in order to improve some of its constituent businesses. The credit for originating Breakthrough within BP was given to the Managing Director of BP Exploration Ltd, who had an M.B.A. from Stanford University and was a protege of Pascale. BP use JMW as its Breakthrough consultants, in a similar role to that of Charles Smith at Rover, but JMW appear to be more visible, supporting and helping to manage the company's Breakthrough projects. At the same time, JMW's lack of specialist technological knowledge has probably ensured that BP itself was responsible for most of the details of its Breakthrough programme. One BP executive admitted that 'there was a lot of scepticism around the place when these guys arrived, this was removed in a matter of days when people realised they were educators getting us to see things we don't normally see'.[42] Whether or not Breakthrough really has generated success or rejuvenation at BP is not to be proved either way, but there is a feeling within the organisation, reflected upon by one manager, that it has 'more to do with changing peoples behaviours and relationships to one another, and is orientated towards human factors rather than pound notes'.[43] It is useful that the way Pascale's ideas were transferred, through the network of management consultants into Rover and BP, has been recorded in some detail. There appears to be scant previous documentation of the powerful impact that management consultants have had on innovation diffusion, particularly in the UK; but their work should not be overlooked in any future work on the acquisition of competitive capability.

At the time of the advent of Breakthrough in Rover, the willingness to utilise external help meant that other consultants could be used to support moves designed to protect Rover from Honda. Approaches were made by senior manufacturing personnel, including Barr, to Professor Dan Jones at Cardiff University, to Bill Conway and Hal Mather, the US-based manufacturing gurus, and to the European motor industry analysts Ludwigson & Associates, for information and consultancy advice. Rover's discovery that it actually had things in common with other organisations was shown in the way that a sizeable proportion of Rover's planning managers took, almost fervently, to reading certain relevant texts. One example is the book *The Machine that Changed the World*, the report of the IMVP (International Motor Vehicle Program, based at MIT in America) study of automotive manufacturing already referred to in Chapter 2.[44] A pre-publication copy of this was sent to Simpson for his approval. Because of the book's relevance to several of the Breakthrough projects, and the way that the book presented the lean production methodology as a possible way forward, it came to be treated almost as a company handbook. Copies were sent to every senior manager in the company, further evidence of the attempt to move away from the fear that outside influences which had prevailed at Rover since the formation of the monolithic BL in the 1970s.

Whereas the conceptual sources for the Breakthrough policies are rather obscure, the findings of the International Motor Vehicle Programme (IMVP) centred at MIT are well known in the industry. More recent developments, in association with Arthur Anderson Consultants, have extended the application of the concept of lean-production into the supply chain through benchmarking studies. Rover has itself undertaken a process of benchmarking. The Benchmarking programme was instigated at Rover by the Quality Strategy Director, following widespread publicising of the method by several of the larger management consultancy firms. Benchmarking is an attempt to establish what practices distinguish weak companies from strong ones. It can be applied equally to overall strategies and to specific operations, but, clearly, organisations with a *world-class* record are taken as examples to emulate. Once the benchmark is made, it is possible to identify differences between weak and strong systems, and learning, but not necessarily copying, the strong company's approach in order to eliminate the weakness.[45] Despite the efforts of the company's Quality Strategy and Manufacturing Strategy departments, Rover has not pursued its benchmarking activity enthusiastically. This may indeed be something that is inherent in the benchmarking process itself, which lends itself to the presentation of incomplete explanations of how the performance levels are achieved. It is easy to quote figures from *world-class* firms without understanding competitors' processes or management practices, and this led to the making of several important decisions on a primarily factional basis. The importance of benchmarking was, it seemed, not that the measures were accurate, but that they created the political conditions and the pressure for change. An example of this is the decision to try to reduce the number of company staff to the same proportional levels found in the world-class Honda and Toyota organisations. One of the fundamental weaknesses of the world-class benchmarking studies is that they do not allow for differences in vertical integration, or disintegration, of production. As an example, Rover cannot emulate the Japanese practice of relying on supplier companies to undertake a significant amount of the design and development work for new models, in addition to the higher levels of bought-in components from the supply chain. In these cases, an apparent difference in physical productivity turns out to be illusory because Japanese companies undertake less of the work in-house, and require less employment to finish off one unit of output. Japanese firms are not more productive in this respect; they have just decided to do less of the work in their own factories.

The adoption of Breakthrough at Rover was triggered by the appointment of a new managing director. This follows the pattern of the successful rejuvenations examined by Stopford and Baden-Fuller, who noted that four of the six organisations analysed in their studies had appointed a new CEO just before the adoption of the programme. The other two had undergone radical changes of priorities, away from financial pressures and towards a longer-term vision,[46] which in its effect is much the same as having a new man in place. If the Rover Breakthrough is to be a success, it is a matter of some concern that its introduction was not due to, and has not resulted in, such a change of intent in the Rover organisation. This is illustrated by the repeated requests from the executive committee for financial evaluation information from the Breakthrough projects. Rover's Breakthrough approach also differs from Stopford and Baden-Fuller's rejuvenation model in that it was introduced after being 'sold' to the chief executive. Stopford and Baden-Fuller were unable to determine the exact cause of the changes in their rejuvenated organisations; but they are clear that the external pressures and changes in markets which generated the rejuvenations were very pressing and were experienced by the whole organisation. It is Stopford and Baden-Fuller's belief that the appreciation of the pressures by the entire organisation cause rejuvenation under the guidance of the CEO.[47] In Rover's case, the pressures leading to the adoption of Breakthrough were not perceived by the organisation as a whole, but only by a few individuals. Rover's modest success up to privatisation (see Table 5.3), following new model introductions and reasonable financial performance after years of disappointment, generated the false impression that the company had already made the turnaround.

The problem with the indicators in Table 5.3 is that they represent a particular moment in Rover's history, and do not show whether the tide was ebbing or flowing. Some of the results are tainted by poor product planning within the company; for example, miscalculation of the potential markets for Rover 200 and Land Rover Discovery. The profit figures are also somewhat misleading, as they include proceeds from the sale of assets, such as the Land Rover Parts operation, the remaining shares in the IT firm ISTEL, and the sale of land at the Cowley plant and the Canley site to BAe. Nor could the firm expect to maintain high sales figures for the Montego and Maestro. Similarly, the recession hit Rover just as hard as the rest of the UK motor industry, which saw new car sales for the first six months of 1991 up to 30 per cent below those of 1990. Rover worked alternate-week production on its Rover 800 model, extended the summer shutdown by an extra third and reduced the production of most of its models in order to reduce its losses. These pressures, instead of promoting strategic thought in the company and the renewed support of Breakthrough, are making its executives embark on major cost reduction exercises to try and avert disaster; for example, the closure of the company's Sterling subsidiary in the USA. The Breakthrough rejuvenation at Rover has not yet begun to happen, and the evidence presented above suggests it is unlikely that it ever will.

Table 5.3
Pre-Privatisation Highlights, 1991

Launch of a new Rover 800 model

Metro, Rover 200, 400 and Discovery all winning *What Car?* awards

Buoyant sales of the ageing Montego and Maestro models

Lengthy waiting lists for Rover 200 models and Land Rover Discovery

Insufficient capacity for the high demand of the new 'K' series engine

Profit for first half 1990 at £33m.[48]

Increasing market share despite 22% drop in TIV (Total Industry Volume)

Source: Rover internal publication, '1991 Financial Results'.

The Rover Group's approach to its relationship with Honda, and the dependence which has developed in design and manufacturing capability (see Chapter 3) were not addressed by the company's Breakthrough initiative. Honda was involved in Rover's attempted Breakthrough, but only because of its role as one of Rover's most important material suppliers, not because of its status as the source of most of Rover's manufacturing and product technology. The

Breakthrough initiative reflects Rover's desire to survive as an automotive manufacturer by attempting to generate an organisation capable of funding its own technological developments and new products. Breakthrough was introduced to Rover following the appointment of a new MD who was persuaded to adopt the approach by a firm of US management consultants. Networks of such consultants exist as a previously uninvestigated but demonstrably powerful means of innovation diffusion. Rover's Breakthrough did not generate the scale of reform or rejuvenation that was hoped for. This failure can be laid at the door of some of the most influential factions in the company; but it is also in part due to the organisation's inability to change its operating practices. Breakthrough was successful in creating a rhetoric of change, but the reality did not match up to the rhetoric. In any case, as the position of Rover both financially and in the market continued to deteriorate, it found itself in a position where it was managing the business against a backdrop of decline. It was not that the Rover company was incapable of making the promised transitions; it was just that the structural conditions within which change has to take place could not be maintained. In the end the company managed transition, but it was not the sort of productive and financial transition promised by the Breakthrough strategy. Rover's management understands that transition, in these circumstances, equals more job losses in order to protect profits and cash flow.

Notes

1. J. Womack, D. Jones and D. Roos, *The Machine that Changed the World* (New York, 1990), p. 173.
2. J.M. Stopford and C. Baden-Fuller, 'Corporate Rejuvenation', *Journal of Management Studies*, Vol. 27 No. 4 (July 1990), p. 401.
3. P. Crosby, *Quality is Free* (New York, 1979).
4. W.E. Deming, *Out of Crisis: Quality, Productivity and Competitive Position* (Cambridge, 1986).
5. P.F. Drucker, *Innovation and Entrepreneurship: Practice and Principles* (London, 1985); idem, *The Frontiers of Management* (New York, 1986).
6. E. Goldratt, *The Goal* (Aldershot, 1984).
7. P. Grinyer, D. Mayes and P. McKiernan, *Sharpbenders: The Secrets of Unleashing Corporate Potential* (Oxford, 1988).

8. R.H. Hayes and S.C. Wheelwright, *Restoring Our Competitive Edge* (New York, 1984); R.H. Hayes, S.C. Wheelwright and K. Clark, *Dynamic Manufacturing* (London, 1988).
9. K. Imai, *Kaizen: The Key to Japan's Competitive Success* (New York, 1986).
10. J.M. Juran, *Quality Planning and Analysis* (New York, 1970); idem, *Juran on Planning for Quality* (New York, 1988).
11. R.M. Kanter, *The Change Masters* (London, 1985); idem, *When Giants Learn to Dance* (London, 1990).
12. J. Kay, *Foundations of Corporate Success: How Business Strategies Add Value* (Oxford, 1993).
13. H. Mather, *Competitive Manufacturing* (Englewood Cliffs, NJ, 1988).
14. K. Ohmae, *The Mind of the Strategist* (New York, 1982).
15. T. Ohno, *Toyota Production System* (Tokyo, 1988).
16. R.T. Pascale, *Managing on the Edge* (New York, 1990).
17. T. Peters and R.H. Waterman, *In Search of Excellence* (New York, 1982); T. Peters and N. Austin, *A Passion for Excellence* (London, 1985); T. Peters, *Thriving on Chaos* (London, 1989).
18. M.E. Porter, *Cases in Competitive Strategy* (New York, 1983); idem, *Competitive Advantage* (New York, 1985); idem, *The Competitive Advantage of Nations* (London, 1990).
19. R.J. Schonberger, *Japanese Manufacturing Techniques* (New York, 1982); idem, *World Class Manufacturing* (New York, 1986).
20. S. Shingo, *Study of Toyota Production System* (Norwalk, OH, 1981); idem, *S.M.E.D., a Revolution in Manufacturing* (Cambridge, MA, 1985).
21. W. Skinner, *Manufacturing in the Corporate Strategy* (New York, 1984); idem, *Manufacturing, the Formidable Competitive Weapon* (New York, 1985).
22. O. Wight, *M.R.P.* (Boston, MA, 1971); G. Plossl, *Production and Inventory Control* (New York, 1967).
23. Peters and Waterman, *In Search of Excellence*.
24. Pascale, *The Edge*, p. 16.
25. H. Mintzberg, *Mintzberg on Management* (New York, 1987), p. 95.
26. Subsequently recorded in Pascale, *The Edge*.
27. Interview with BP Executive (AD), Sept. 1990.
28. R.H. Schaffer, *The Breakthrough Strategy* (New York, 1988).
29. Ibid., p. 74.
30. Imai, *Kaizen*.
31. Schaffer, *Breakthrough Strategy*, p. 61.
32. Ibid., p. 19.
33. Ibid.
34. Ibid., p. 102.
35. D. Miller and P. Friesen, *Organisations: A Quantum View* (London, 1984), p. 87.
36. H. Mintzberg, *Structure in Fives: Designing Effective Organisations* (London, 1983).
37. Miller and Friesen, *Quantum View*, p. 202.
38. Interview with G. Day, March 1989.
39. R. Bertodo, 'Evolution of an Engineering Organization', *International Journal of Technology Management*, Vol. 3 No. 6 (1988), pp. 693-710.

40. G. Hamel and C.K. Prahalad, 'Strategic Intent', *Harvard Business Review*, Vol. 67 No. 3 (May-June 1989), p. 63.
41. Ibid., p. 64.
42. Interview with BP Manager (AD), Sept. 1990.
43. Interview with BP Central Planning Manager (CW), Sept. 1990.
44. Womack, Jones and Roos, *The Machine that Changed the World*.
45. R.C. Camp, *Benchmarking: The Search for Industry Best Practices that Lead to Superior Performance* (Milwaukee, WI, 1989).
46. J.M. Stopford and C. Baden-Fuller, 'Corporate Rejuvenation', *Journal of Management Studies*, Vol. 27 No. 4 (July 1990).
47. Ibid., p. 404.
48. *Independent*, 17 Sept. 1990, p. 23.

6

Examples of Success

The highlights for the last year for me were, in no particular order: the acquisition by BMW which was a major endorsement of Rover's achievements, our sales growth in markets outside the UK, and associated production increases and new jobs, the launch of the new Range Rover, and the winning of the prestigious UK Quality Award. We can do better, and with attention to areas such as attendance and our continuing need to provide even higher levels of quality and prestige in our cars, we gain even more.
John Towers, Rover Chief Executive, 1995[1]

In Chapter 5 we described a company which was searching for a managerial solution to the problems the company was facing. The company flirted with the importation of Japanese management systems and the use of external consultants and benchmarking exercises. Overall, these managerial techniques could not turn the business around, because at heart it was always unsound. Market share of the company's home market was steadily lost, and the core car business was never able to generate a substantial surplus of cash. Limited cash was always going to be a problem, because the firm's ability to invest in new processes and products. As Williams and others note, the Rover Group suffered from the age-old problem of BLMC, that of generating little or no cash from each unit sold.[2] In these circumstances, the business strategy should never have been to rush into projects, but, more cautiously, to make the best of limited resources. Indeed, in a number of specific cases Rover management did just that. Rover managed to stretch the use of the K-series engine across the model range, and with 'Rover tomorrow' the policy was change what could be changed within the existing framework of labour relations, rather than demolish and rebuild.

Rover can be justly proud of two reportedly home grown developments: the K-series engine, and changes to working practices dubbed 'Rover Tomorrow — The New Deal'. These successes are rightly cited as being at the heart of the firm's rejuvenation and tell the world that Rover has changed from its troubled days in the 1970s into a modern innovative automobile company. But these examples are isolated and non-representative. And even here further investigation shows the large and powerful hand of Honda directing the activity.

The K-series engine (launched in 1993 as a 1.1 and 1.4 litre with a 1.6 and 1.8 added in 1995, and a V6 due for launch in 1996) is at the heart of most of Rover's new small and medium models (Rover 100, 200, 400) and has won several awards, including the Design Council award for environmental features in 1991. The engine, when coupled to the R65 gearbox licensed from Peugeot, has provided Rover with a power-train which has brought the company to a competitive level in the class (see Table 6.1). The K-series story represents in microcosm the whole turnaround in Rover's fortunes.[3] The engine is manufactured at Longbridge and used in Longbridge vehicles, but though typical in many ways of that part of the firm, it also shows the influence of the parent firm's technostructure.

Table 6.1
Comparison of K-Series Engine

Engine	BHP	Torque
Rover K 1.4 16v	95	91
Honda Civic 16v	90	82
Nissan Sunny 1.4 16v	83	82
Suzuki 1.3 16v injection	101	83

Source: Car (Oct. 1989).

Development of the K-series was a clear strategy for the firm to follow in the 1970s, as its other engines were antiquated to the point of being ruled illegal by increasingly stringent emission regulations. The company still relied on the 1952 A-series (1100cc and 1275cc) developed originally for Austin and used in the Mini, Metro, Maestro and Montego vehicles (still used in the Mini and Metro automatic in 1995; see Plate 6.1), and the O-series and S-series (recently updated to T-series) (1.6 and 2.0 litre) engines, developed from the 1960s B-series. The plans to develop a new engine were formed in the 1970s, but the diversion of resources into the 1977-81 Metro project and the late-running LM10/11 (Maestro and Montego) projects pushed the programme back many years, with the result that work did not finally start until 1984. The advent of the K-series engine, and its timing following the start of collaboration with Honda, marked the introduction to the firm of modern ways of product development. Rover, like much of the rest of the car industry, was accustomed to a cycle of product development in which design and engineering were dealt with separately from manufacturing. In consequence, designs might be produced that the facilities could not cope with, necessitating either a change in design or an adaptation of the facilities, a waste, whichever compromise was chosen. The new approach, termed simultaneous engineering or concurrent design, relies on combining the tasks of manufacturing, engineering and product design to optimise the total project.[4]

The K-series also saw Rover using another significant development in automotive design management of the 1980s: supply chain involvement strategies. The car makers' traditional approach to design was to treat a project as highly sensitive and secret, to the point of not allowing suppliers to gain an overview of the concept, in case the opposition were to hear about it. This may have allowed companies to steal a march on competitors, but has been proved to be expensive in terms of product quality and cost; lack of co-ordination leads to overstretching of resources and the use of designers working on many different elements and systems at the same time, instead of being able to specialise. The modern approach is to include the suppliers of a part as members of the design team. It is clear, after all, that the design staff at the firm who make components, having designed many similar parts for many years, know the manufacturing process and specialised technology used in

producing the best components. Bringing the suppliers into the design teams can cut the costs and lead times of parts greatly, by effectively increasing the number of design specialists at no extra cost to the vehicle manufacturer. It also extends the principle of simultaneous engineering to the supply network, with all the gains in terms of cost, quality and time that this brings. Rover worked very closely with the key suppliers in the K-programme. The value of these links is clearly evident in the K-series, in which the development of the technology needed for the engine depended on the supply network.[5]

The K-series included several new or state-of-the-art ideas, including a move to 16-valve engine technology.[6] Traditional engine design used one valve each for the fuel and air mixture going in and exhaust gases going out. Modern engines use two or even more valves for each part of the cycle to improve the speed and efficiency of the operation, and thus increase the power of the engine. K-series was designed primarily as a 16-valve engine with a lower powered eight-valve model also developed for use in smaller vehicles. Both variants of the engine have an aluminium cylinder block and head. These need less coolant than traditional cast-iron designs because of the conductive properties of aluminium. As a result the engine warms up quickly, enabling it to run at its greatest efficiency for longer periods of time. Aluminium engines are also lighter, so that the vehicles carrying them require less power to produce the same performance. Although this was not the first use of aluminium in the industry, it did reflect the current trend.

Another innovative manufacturing practice in the K-series family of engines is sandwich construction. In a conventional engine, many separate bolts are used to fasten the head, crank casings, sump, and so on to the main cylinder block. The K-series, by contrast, uses ten precision steel bolts running through the entire engine to hold it all together (see Plate 6.2). This, once the technical difficulties of close tolerances and torque settings had been dealt with, reduced the manufacturing complexity of the assembly operation and facilitated the automation of many of the steps involved. The sandwich construction method, in its turn, gave rise to the need to develop new sealant methods to replace traditional gaskets. The manufacturing cycle times meant that a sealant had to be developed which was capable of setting quickly and being applied accurately enough to cope with the tight tolerances created by having thinner walls between delicate oil and water channels. The sealant had also to be able to withstand the higher operating temperatures (150°C instead of 120°C) and the greater thermal shock of the faster warm-up time of the new engine.[7] This development was pioneered by Rover's supplier Loctite, and is now being used by several other manufacturers.

The precision required of the new design and manufacturing techniques demanded a highly accurate method of casting to produce the block and head. Rover adopted the innovative Cosworth low-pressure sand (LPS) injection process, which produces moulds for casting engine components by injecting special sand-resin mixtures into patterns. This technology is still kept secret, and is the subject of some legal rumbling between Rover and its originators, Cosworth Engineering. After negotiations to licence the technique broke down, the firm 'poached' Cosworth engineers and suppliers to replicate the whole process. Mueller argues that this in-house reproduction of the technology caused the project to last three years longer than it would have if the licensing agreement had been pursued.

Honda also introduced Rover to another development in automotive design management which emerged in the 1980s: parts carry-over. Carry-over, as explained in Chapter 2, is the production of parts which can be carried over from one model to its replacement, or which can be used in more than one vehicle.[8] From the opposite view-point, it means that the design of replacement models seeks to accommodate as many parts as possible from its predecessor. The advantages are obvious: the production of a new model requires fewer design staff, so that the process is speeded up, and the part is already tried and tested. Parts carry-over is a skill which Honda has developed over many years. The Honda Concerto, for example, contained more than 70 per cent of the same parts as the Ballade model it replaced. In a typical new Western model, only 30 per cent of parts would be carried over. The level is now rising, as the benefits of this very simple strategy are at last being perceived. Carry-over, as it happens, was not used in the K-series project, which still relied on designing the engine from scratch, but it has been the major factor behind the ever-increasing frequency of model face-lifts.

The effects of Honda's introduction of simultaneous engineering, supplier integration and parts carry-over have been responsible for

Plate 6.2 The Longbridge K-Series Assembly Line, 1990s

Rover's increased activity in product development. It is not clear whether Rover engineers have mastered all the complexities of a fully modern design strategy, and it is unlikely that this is an area where the link to BMW will strengthen the expertise. BMW have, in common with the other German manufacturers, very long design processes of more than five years for designing a new model, unlike the Japanese, who now measure theirs in months with around 30 being normal. Such approaches to shortening the product design cycle are now accepted as common sense. The primary motivation for creating shorter design cycles was the need for the emerging Japanese firms of the 1960s to exert their influence on the highly competitive Japanese home market. At that time, it was usual to replace models every few years rather than the ten years or longer which had become the pattern in Europe during the 1960s and 1970s. The arrival of the Japanese in Europe, after they had radically restructured the US market, has forced the native players in the market to adopt new approaches to design. It is no longer good enough to have a technologically advanced product: it must be fashionable as well.

This is clearly something which Rover has been forced to accept as a result of the link with Honda — no other approach would fit with the dominating design process used by Honda for their part — the major part — of the collaborative programmes. From reliance in the 1970s and 1980s on design projects which called for totally new products, the firm has moved to a strategy of more frequent, cosmetic revamping of existing models, and the licensing of major components such as the R65 gear-box. This is clearly a capability that Rover has managed to acquire from Honda. This may be successful in the short term and allow the firm to catch up with its European competitors. But it is far from the complete picture. Rover relies too much on other firms to provide it with core components. These firms are there, not to help Rover become more profitable, but to make money for themselves. Honda, as has been shown, never allowed Rover access to its latest technology, such as the V-TEC engine. Only models and designs which could no longer be exploited as innovatory were made available to Rover, and these at a price. It may have allowed Rover to make up some of the ground lost in the early 1980s, but provided nothing in the way of a launch-pad for future success. Furthermore, at a time when the recession-hit European car industry is having to cut its profit margins to the limit, Rover, by buying in or licensing most of its core components from firms who are making a good profit on them, is contributing to its competitors' profits and adding to its own costs. This is poor economics, and Rover's recent financial performance reflects this. The firm claims its 1993 profits of £56m as a success; but the truth is that these figures, which included an injection of around £100m for the sale of Land Rover Parts to Unipart, still represent a tiny return of just over one per cent on sales. Nor do the annual figures follow any particular pattern; the firm has returned profits and losses almost at random for several years. Nevertheless, the K-series was a remarkable achievement for Rover, given its recent past. It will be interesting to see what design management practices remain, now that the hot-line to Tokyo has gone.

The same success has been claimed by the company for its other major advance in management practices, those on the shop floor. Changes in personnel strategy embodied in 'The New Deal' (the term given by the Rover management to the series of agreements with the union joint negotiating committee and changes in organisation during the 1990s) show an appreciation of Honda's methods without absorbing the skills needed to take full advantage of them. 'The New Deal', or 'Rover Tomorrow', as it has also been called, represents a move by Rover to adopt many of the work organisation and management practices found in Japan, which are widely believed to be the secret of Japanese success in manufacturing industry.

The Rover executive has followed a two-pronged strategy, re-negotiating contracts with employees and also re-organising the management relationships within the firm in the production areas. During the 1970s and 1980s the centre of power in the firm moved away from union shop stewards towards the central executive echelons of the firm. This has often been cited as returning the right to manage to the management, and is seen as Edwardes' biggest success. However, the shift concentrated much of the responsibility for decision-making away from the shop floor, where all the value-adding activities occur, and into the finance and personnel departments. In the late 1980s and early 1990s, responsibility was to some extent returned to those in the production areas of the firm. Each of the manufacturing sites now has a managing director with much more responsibility than the plant directors had in the 1970s. The management of shop floor activities has also been re-defined, with production managers being given most responsibility for the manufacturing process. Each site has a single managing director for operations. He has production directors responsible for the different areas: engines and final assembly. These in turn have managers who have total responsibility for the daily operation of their own part of the process. The finance and personnel departments are now deployed in a supporting capacity to the production managers and directors: 'in essence this was designed to be a much more broadly based personnel role, supporting key line managers within the company with a consultancy service.'[9] Other functions have also been deployed more locally, with product and manufacturing engineering staff reporting to the plant and production line managers.

The new contracts for the shopfloor employees (or associates, as they are now termed) enforce the Total Quality approach which has been introduced through extensive training programmes. The result is that the organisation of the production lines themselves are broken up into relatively autonomous teams of associates (or production cells) who, in conjunction with the local management, have total responsibility for how the work and housekeeping of the cell is organised. Job rotation and quality improvement activities are organised by the team leader (an experienced individual selected by the team and the cell manager). This has a superficial resemblance to the old ways, when the management would make requests to the shop-stewards, who would in turn organise the labour force; but there is one great difference: the pressure on the employees now comes from their workmates, rather than from above. Before, the managers were liable to be blamed if things went wrong, but now the team suffers as a whole, so there is a large degree of peer pressure on the employees.[10] Many of the changes were introduced under the banner of 'the Japanese are coming'[11] with the implication that the company would fold, and everyone become unemployed, if the changes were not introduced.

At the same time as the shopfloor relationships were altered, many other initiatives copied from Japan were introduced. These included company uniforms, supposed to make everyone appear to have the same status; the abolition of reserved car parking for managers, and the removal of other white collar perks such as staff-only canteens. These initiatives were all intended to replace the old hierarchy with a single-status system, where rewards were based on individual contribution and not on title or rank.[12] But the reality is rather different; many of the changes have actually served to strengthen the divisions in the firm: staff and managers have been provided with uniforms of a different quality from those of the shopfloor workers, and often in a different colour, following changes in supply during the introduction of the scheme which targeted management ahead of shopfloor employees; managers who need their cars during the day as part of their job still have reserved car parking spaces; several sites do not admit cars which do not display the corporate car fleet pass (the MVO and Executive car lease schemes); and the ostensibly democratic restaurants are no longer restricted to staff and management, but do not allow employees in dirty overalls and are, furthermore, sited close to the office complexes, away from the production lines. Shopfloor employees frequent the take-away outlets on the factory floor. Finally, the company promised lifetime employment for its employees but this, as we all know, can only be underwritten by corporate financial success; if the future was to be anything like the past then Rover was ill-equipped to make this sort of contract. The promise was made in the context of a flurry of publicity which tried to offer the employees something for surrendering levels of demarcation and precise job definitions for more flexible contracts, but was qualified to mean that employees whose jobs disappear will be offered a certain amount of re-training and would be dismissed if they did not accept. The different parts of Rover have adopted the New Deal in different ways, as befits their respective traditions, existing structures and characters. Land Rover has been slow to develop manufacturing cells and the organisation structure that goes with it, but has introduced teams. Cowley, on the other hand, has a strong cell structure, but the divisions between teams are not as clear as at Longbridge or Solihull.

Rover is motivated to introduce Japanese management practices by the need to emulate the world leaders, but how much of this came from Honda? Mair suggests the role of Nissan in Sunderland was greater than that of Honda, and it is true that several groups of Rover managers visited the North-East of England.[13] There were, however, many more visits to Honda's Ohio and Suzuka factories, and more recent trips to Swindon, following the start of engine and vehicle assembly operations there. The influence of Honda can likewise be seen in Rover's production and material control approaches, and it is hard to agree with Mair's suggestion.

The move in recent years has been towards the system adopted at Longbridge. It is very closely aligned with Honda's production strategy: long and steady build programmes calling for material to be delivered to the side of the tracks using lean production methods. These include a near-JIT approach (see Chapter 2), called minimal inventory control at Rover, which uses a form of *kanban* to pull material from nearby warehousing in response to a relatively inflexible — compared to true *kanban* — build programme established some weeks in advance of manufacture. Some senior manufacturing personnel have for some time seen this as the best approach, but the other parts of the firm have different approaches. At Land Rover, the strategy has been to adopt the so-called Manufacturing Resource Planning (MRPII), which uses computer databases to set production targets according to forecast sales.[14] This is ideally suited to the Solihull site, with its low volume, long lead-time products in strong demand. Cowley, as the remnant of the BL re-organisation, has a material control strategy based on the early work of the BL Systems arm (since renamed and sold off as ISTEL to AT&T) which utilises much information technology to time deliveries to the product schedule, set one week in advance of manufacture. This has recently been brought more into line with the Longbridge system, following the decision to build the Rover 600 in Oxford. The impetus from the central Rover staffs and commercial areas, particularly during the Breakthrough process, was in the direction of a true time-based organisation or JIT system as seen at Toyota and Nissan, incorporating flexible build schedules and *kanban* links back into the supplier network.[15] Using the normal time-span between order and delivery in the UK automotive industry, a time-based organisation would need to deliver a vehicle to order in under three weeks. At present the market is operated with massive stocks of finished vehicles, so that customers generally receive their vehicles in about two weeks, allowing for the transfer of money, delivery from holding compound, preparation and registration. Honda's strategy is not a full JIT system, because it prefers to reduce the variety of vehicles in the market place, so that orders can be satisfied from stock. However, this stock is made in a JIT manner; the amount of material needed to operate the manufacturing process is reduced, and efficiency is increased.

The reduced variety allows the amount of stock needed to cover the range of choices made by the customer to be low.

The conflict between these various strategies and systems became a matter of concern during 1989, when the newly privatised Rover Group adopted BAe's dominant strategy and flirted with centralising the disparate activities of the sub-organisations. This led to the strengthening of many central departments, including personnel, finance and purchasing; and gave rise to much tension, as managers of different departments doggedly tried to protect what they had achieved and developed over many years. Nowhere was the pressure greater than at Land Rover, where the spotlight fell on the increasingly unfashionable MRPII system. The senior managers in the centralised, powerful finance and purchasing organisation, most of whom had previously dealt only with cars, could not understand how the most successful part of the Rover Group could prosper using such an apparently outmoded and inefficient system. MRPII's inherent batching policies, resulting from the need to schedule predetermined capacities through the production facilities, were seen as a wasteful means of operating, particularly compared to the leaner car production control systems which had moved towards *kanban*. They could not see that the high levels of complexity in the Land Rover products, particularly the Defender model, are better suited to the MRPII approach than to JIT.[16] The model production control system for cars, as piloted at Longbridge and later introduced at Cowley, was largely based on the cosmetic introduction of JIT principles achieved by the use of large distribution centres, which held two days' worth of suppliers' stocks. This material is then released to the tracks in a scheduled manner which imitates true JIT, in which the parts would not be made until shortly before they were required. This approach was viewed with some scepticism by Land Rover manufacturing personnel: 'they [cars] have all the inventory in a warehouse just down the road.'[17] The intention of the cars' JIT programme (called minimum inventory control: MIC) was to remove the stock from the track-side, into the warehouse, followed by a stock reduction programme. This, however, has not been widely implemented. A recent modification has been the introduction of the Distribution Efficiency programme, which toyed with the idea of introducing a full JIT system, but was stopped by the vested interests of the different factions in the company. The programme has managed to introduce a better method of finished vehicle stock control, which allows Rover to control the flow of vehicles into the dealer network and so divert them to customers wanting the vehicle. In the past, the vehicles were built for a particular retailer, and there was no mechanism for matching customers with vehicles which were not available at their own particular outlet. The programme also saw a rationalisation of the models offered to customers. Orders from customers whose requirements could not be met out of stock were placed on a 'factory orders only' list, with a 13-week lead time. In fact, since before the changes, if the dealer did not have the particular vehicle in stock, an order was made to the factory which took about 13 weeks to process, the difference for the customer was not apparent; but there is less need for the smaller dealers to hold stocks of many different vehicles.

The Land Rover system was a complex adoption and enhancement of an off-the-shelf manufacturing resource planning (MRPII) software and materials management system produced by IBM. To get this system running had been a long task, occupying many man-years of Land Rover's and ISTEL's resources. It was seen by those involved as an innovative way of dealing with the peculiarities of Land Rover's manufacturing and sales activities. However, it was seen from outside as a half-introduced, out-dated and costly bureaucratic minefield. There was great pressure to drop MRPII and follow the pseudo-JIT systems being pursued in the rest of the group. But the imposition of such a change was fiercely resisted.

The product supply reorganisation of 1990 re-established a decentralised Rover organisation, thereby re-creating Land Rover as an independently functioning operation. Informal strategies were developed which were intended to protect and enhance the existing MRPII systems. One such was produced by the same core of personnel who introduced the original MRPII initiative,[18] and sought to preserve the MRPII systems. They also believed they should convince the cars organisation that an MRP-based approach is required for it, too, to gain control of its production operations: 'MRP is the road to pursue and that Land Rover are to become a reference of what could be achieved in the future by the Group'.[19]

The establishment of a centralised Rover Group purchasing department in 1989 has now been confirmed as a temporary measure. The primary task of the purchasing director appointed in March 1991 was to manage a move towards a totally decentralised purchasing role.[20] This role would be played by the engineers designing the new vehicles and the newly established logistics departments within each of the manufacturing plants, or business units, as part of the restructuring in 'the New Deal'. The MRPII approach at Land Rover may have survived these early storms, but the clear interest of BMW in building a capable four-wheel-drive presence in the growing and highly profitable market will probably renew the pressure. Land Rover, the jewel of the group, would on its own have justified the price paid by BMW for the entire firm. The future aspirations of BMW for Land Rover are still unclear, but it must surely be at the heart of BMW's strategic plans, plans which would probably see Land Rover expanding to dominate a fast growing market. Such an expansion would need the adoption of production techniques more suited to efficient volume manufacturing, and the accompanying rejection of MRPII. BMW must manage this change carefully if Land Rover people are to make it work. The car-manufacturing side of the business has a Japanese installed JIT-based system, and was probably thought by BMW to be a valuable tool for finding out just how it really works. But Rover's approach is an adaptation of Honda's approach to European supply practices, and is therefore not a true JIT system. Honda's system is flexible day-by-day, but is based on stable, long-term production plans. Rover's method may have led to increased efficiency by increasing material throughput and turnover, but it does not contain the elements which have been hardest for Western firms to learn about: managing the supply chain in a JIT manner and the development of production flexibility, and the ordering of management tools so as to respond quickly to customer demand.

This chapter has sought to establish the truth behind some of the headlines proclaiming Rover's recent change in fortunes, the K-series and 'Rover Tomorrow — The New Deal'. The impetus behind both of these, and the changes in material control systems were a direct result of the Honda-Rover partnership. The fundamental problem was that these particular successes did not carry enough weight to turn the Rover Group around. The joint venture was expected to achieve this, but the underlying fundamentals were still much the same in the early 1990s as they were in the 1980s. In any case, the history of the Rover company tells us a different story in which successive eras of management actions and management styles failed to restore the company fortunes and the question remains open as to why we should have expected more from the Honda-Rover joint venture.

Notes

1. J. Towers (Rover Group Chief Executive), *Report for Associates 1994* (Rover internal publication, 1995).
2. K. Williams, C. Haslam, S. Johal and J. Williams, *Cars: Analysis, History, Cases* (Oxford, 1994).
3. For a description of the technology involved in the project see F. Mueller, 'The Role of Know-How in Corporate Rejuvenation: The Case of Rover', *Business Strategy Review,* Vol. 4 No. 3 (Autumn 1993), p. 15-24.
4. K. Clark and T. Fujimoto, *Product Development Performance: Strategy, Organisation, and Management in the World Auto Industry* (Boston, MA, 1991).
5. F. Muller, 'A New Engine of Change in Employee Relationships', *Personnel Management,* Vol. 23 No. 7 (July 1991), pp. 30-3.
6. R. Stone, D. Crabb, R. Richardson and A. Draper, 'The Design and Development of the Rover K16 Engine', *Procedures of the Institute of Mechanical Engineers,* Vol. 204 No. 4 (1990), pp. 221-36.
7. J. Barrett, 'Sealant Offers High-Temperature Solution', *Eureka,* Vol. 10 No. 6 (1990), pp. 24-7.
8. This is termed robust design and the effects can lead to a family of successful products. See K. Rothwell and J. Gardiner, 'The Role of Design in Product and Process Change', *Design Studies,* Vol .4 No. 3 (1983), pp. 161-9; and J. Gardiner, 'Robust and Lean Designs with State of the Art Automotive and Aircraft Examples', in C. Freeman (ed.), *Design, Innovation and Long Cycles in Economic Development* (London, 1986), Ch. 8.
9. D. Bower (Rover Personnel Director), 'Rover Gears up for Success through People', internal reprint of published article but with no bibliographic information provided (1992).
10. For a discussion of the different motivational factors in Japanese management techniques, see P. Garahan and P. Stewart, *The Nissan Enigma: Flexibility at Work in a Local Economy* (London, 1992); P. Wickens, *The Road to Nissan: Flexibility, Quality, Teamwork* (London, 1987); M. Parker and J. Slaughter, *Choosing Sides: Unions and the Team Concept* (Boston, MA, 1988).
11. Presentation by John Towers, Rover's Chief Executive, to every employee as part of roadshow in 1992.
12. J. Towers (Rover Managing Director), 'A New Deal?', *Manufacturing Engineer* (July 1992), pp. 45-7.
13. See A. Mair, *Honda's Global Local Corporation* (Basingstoke, 1994), Ch. 13.
14. MRPII (manufacturing resource planning) is an approach developed by IBM in the 1950s which relies on using computer databases to schedule the factory following economic batch quantities to achieve a production schedule based on a sales forecast. For an overview see any Production and Operations Management textbook, for

example, R. Markland, S. Vickery and R. Davis, *Operations Management: Concepts in Manufacturing and Services* (St. Paul, MN, 1995), Ch. 13; and for a more detailed description see O. Wight, *MRPII: Unlocking America's Productivity Potential* (New York, 1981) or J. Orlicky, *Materials Requirements Planning* (New York, 1975).
15. For a description of the differences in JIT approach used by the major automobile manufacturers see A. Pilkington, 'Japanese Production Strategies and Competitive Success: Mazda's Quiet Revolution', *Journal of Far Eastern Business,* Vol. 1 No. 4 (1995), pp. 15-35.
16. S.A. Melnyke and R.S. Gonzalez, 'MRPII: The Early Returns Are In', *Production and Inventory Management* (Q1, 1985), pp. 124-37.
17. Interview with Land Rover PMC (Production and Material Control) Manager (MC), April 1989.
18. Ibid., repeated by a Land Rover PMC Director (PB), May 1989.
19. Interview with Senior Land Rover Manufacturing Manager (DH), April 1989.
20. Interview with Rover Purchasing Director (IR), May 1991.

7

Innovation Roadblock or Gateway?

> *Management observers frequently claim that small organizations are more innovative than larger ones. But is this commonplace necessarily true? Some large enterprises are highly innovative. How do they do it? Can lessons from these companies and their smaller counterparts help other companies become more innovative?*
>
> J.B. Quinn[1]

The history of Rover cars maps out the changing fortunes of a business which, at every stage of its steady decline, has tried the latest innovation in the hope that this would pull it back from the brink. In the business world, many successes have been the result of good luck rather than good management, though many business commentators are charitably inclined to see the two as much the same thing. So it has been with Rover and Land Rover. These two parts of the one company are in sharply contrasting states; Rover is struggling to hold on to volume sales, whilst Land Rover is running an order book and has a waiting list. It is always easier to manage innovation in a business which is cash rich, and Land Rover is certainly the most valuable contributor to the Rover Group's accounts. Where Rover Group managers cannot find funds for development of new models and improvements in its processes, Land Rover's managers find little or no shortages for the improvements they want to make.

Many innovations require routine exploration which is time consuming, labour intensive and a drain on the financial resources of a business. The problem for BMW is how to find funds to cross-subsidise Rover's requirements for product and process development. This raises a set of subsidiary questions:

1. Does Rover have the innovative ability to compete in the global market, or will BMW constantly have to come to its aid, with the

huge financial and practical problems this presents?

2. How capable is Rover of developing independent competitive strategies? Will the declared aim of BMW to leave it a near-independent unit be thwarted, and in the end leave Rover indistinguishable from the rest of BMW — the two-model, small car manufacturing business unit — a German transplant operation assembling cheap cars in Britain, like the Japanese giants?

3. Will any strategies developed in Britain be successful? Rover was always limited by the fact that its size and internal workings rendered impossible the level of investment needed to carry off ambitious strategies. Even down-sizing was a strategy that was hard to implement. What might come of ambitions to become an arm of a global market leader?

The answers to these questions can best be arrived at by studying how innovation in the firm has developed, the status and current strategies of the automotive industry and the place of BMW within that framework.

Much has been written about what makes innovation successful and how the resulting ideas are taken up by other organisations for subsequent development and usage; but much of this work avoids the difficulty of developing a coherent theory by advocating what may be termed a contingency view of innovation — the argument that, since the success of innovation is dependent on many factors, no straightforward and satisfactory theory of innovation is possible. Freeman,[2] for example, identified ten characteristics of successful innovating firms (Table 7.1).

The debate covering cause and effect — contingency — within the process of innovation has developed for several decades, since it was recognised in the early, influential studies of Schumpeter and Jewkes as an essential feature of technology development.[3] These were supplemented by further studies by March and Simon, Burns and Stalker, Woodward, and others[4]. This body of literature has developed into an orthodoxy — a mainstream theory of innovation — which tends to treat innovation as a 'black box'[5] or linear process following a predictable course: problem definition and idea generation; invention; research & development; application or first use; and diffusion.[6] This linear model generated several theories on specific stages of the process — Rogers's model of diffusion is one — and encouraged empirical studies of innovation success.[7] Rogers developed a now widely-established model of what he termed diffusion. The process is important because it determines how innovations emerge, become transmitted and subsequently developed. 'We can define diffusion as the process by which (1) an innovation (2) is communicated through certain channels (3) over time (4) among the members of a social system.'[8] Although this theory has attracted a certain degree of criticism,[9] it can help in understanding the capabilities of Rover because it can be used to explain how the different constituents, internal processes and routines within the firm encourage or deter innovation.

Table 7.1
Freeman's Ten Characteristics of Successful Innovating Firms

1	Strong in-house professional Research & Development
2	Basic research or close connections with those conducting such research
3	The use of patents to gain protection and to bargain with competitors
4	Large enough size to finance heavy R & D expenditure over long periods
5	Shorter lead times than competitors
6	Readiness to take high risks
7	Early and imaginative identification of potential markets
8	Careful attention to the potential market and substantial efforts to involve, educate and assist users
9	Entrepreneurship strong enough effectively to co-ordinate R & D, production and marketing
10	Good communications with the outside scientific world as well as customers

Source: C. Freeman, *The Economics of Industrial Innovation* (Cambridge, MA, 1982), p. 112.

The subject of innovation received renewed attention as a result of investigations like those of Abernathy and Cusumano into the rapid Japanese penetration of US auto and electronics markets.[10] Their studies presented the Japanese firms as being highly competent in taking on ideas from other firms and adapting them to suit their own operations. This leads to apparently innovative products which actually contain little new technology, but bring together different, already available, techniques in a highly effective way. These skills were displayed in full measure by the Japanese car industry, particularly in the areas of model design and alternative manufacturing systems. They stem from the organisations' innovation capabilities, which enabled them to use existing technology and develop highly efficient manufacturing systems.

The Japanese companies were able to achieve re-invention, or the tailoring of innovation to meet specific needs.[11] In the US, Abernathy showed that these re-specified products were able to rejuvenate established market sectors by creating new fashions in technology. The rejuvenation was represented in Abernathy and Utterbeck's technology life-cycle model as a shift away from unspectacular, incremental production development back to a stress on what is new in product development and technological (or, as Abernathy and Utterbeck termed it, major) innovation.[12] The integration of innovation with the demands of the market has emerged as critical, not only to the theorists, but also as the only worthwhile strategy available to the motor industry of the 1990s. All manufacturers have woken up to the truth that success can not come from leadership in one field, be it cost, quality, performance, technology, or fashion. A combination of at least two of these is needed for today's global markets, as the US and European volume manufacturers are rapidly recognising.

But how can firms generate the levels of capability to compete? Japanese firms do not pursue all areas of competitive advantage, as Western firms often do. The trick appears to be to concentrate on core competencies: Honda is recognised for consistency in quality, performance and technology through its extensive engineering capability, Mazda has chosen quality, performance and fashion,[13] whilst Toyota leads the field in cost and quality management. The core fields of expertise of the different firms have not been created as independent strategies, but owe a great deal both to the way the firms developed, and to the demands of the market, which, as we have already seen is highly influential. The observed differences between the different parts of the Rover Group — Land Rover, Cowley, Longbridge and the central staffs areas — illustrate the existence of contingent specificity in the UK firm. That is to say, each organisation has a unique way of configuring itself for innovation, and the different parts of Rover therefore show differing results. This can be observed in the various material management methods adopted by each of the manufacturing sites in Rover, and the exploration in the previous chapter of the K-series engine programme and the introduction of 'Rover Tomorrow — The New Deal'.

The findings of these isolated but detailed investigations have been supported by a brief study of recent changes in the shopfloor techniques at Rover Group conducted in 1992. The study highlights the different approaches to innovation found in the individual parts of the organisation and provides a valuable insight into the present ability of the firm to generate the innovation needed to survive and prosper in the modern car industry. The innovations (see Table 7.2) were examined by interviewing many managers in the central Group Engineering and the Manufacturing Engineering managers at the individual manufacturing plants.[14]

Table 7.2
Innovations Studied in the Rover Group in 1992

Automated Guided Vehicles for LR V8	Minimal Inventory Control — Rover
FMS for Cylinder Heads	MRPII Production Control Systems at Land Rover (IBM COPICS adaptation)
CNC LR Pulley Machining	MRPII Enhancement with CAPP
CNC Flywheel Machining Incorporating Robot Loading	SCOPE Production Sequencing System
Robotics in Chassis Welding (Solihull)	EDI (data interchange) integrated with COPICS
Land Rover Automated Stores	PROSPECTS Bill of Materials

Paint Shop Electronic Tagging Systems	Hot Melt Adhesive Spray at Solihull
Service Parts Processing Capabilities for Land Rover Parts	Laser Door Open Detection in Solihull Final Assembly
Rolling Road for 4x4 ABS System Tests	CNC Hobbing of Gears at Solihull
Vehicle Electrical Testing Systems	Robotics for Body in White
Range Rover Mini Paint Rectification	Order File Cars Order Control System
Final Inspection Data Collection System for Land Rover	Cell Management (The New Deal)
Hydraulic Ride Simulator at Solihull	Total Quality Initiative
TARDIS Personnel and Payment System	Laser Body Measurement at Cowley
Introducing Automated Paint Spraying	Engine 'Stuff' at Longbridge from Honda
R8 Glazing Cell at Longbridge	Robotic Water Leak Testing
CAD System Input from Clay Models	FMS Introduction in Power Train

Source: A. Pilkington, 'A Study of Strategy Formulation in an Automotive Manufacturer' (Unpublished Ph.D. thesis, University of Aston in Birmingham, 1991).

The data were examined using two criteria: the source of the innovation's introduction to the respective part of the company; and the originality of the innovation. The criteria were chosen in the belief that much of what Rover's management thought to be innovative (that is, developed solely for Rover's use) was in fact already being used elsewhere, and was normal in other UK automotive manufacturers. But whether or not innovations were truly innovations, they were included in the study according to their influence on shopfloor operations and the degree of novelty claimed for them by the interviewees.

Closer investigation showed that the vast majority of the innovations had actually been introduced into the company from external organisations (such as Honda and Warwick University) and equipment suppliers. The results of the studies of innovation within the Rover Group are summarised in Table 7.3. There was little difference between the innovative capabilities of the volume production plants (Longbridge and Cowley are combined in the table of results), but the relatively low volume Land Rover organisation at Solihull had significantly more citations, tending to confirm the assertion that innovation is at the heart of success in the car industry, with Land Rover's fortunes resulting to some degree from its greater propensity for innovation than other parts of the group.

Table 7.3
Summary of Study into Innovation in the Rover Group

	Land Rover	Rover Cars
Internal source	3	0
External source	25	14
Innovative	3	2
Non-original	25	12
Total identified	28	14

Source: A. Pilkington, 'A Study of Strategy Formulation in an Automotive Manufacturer' (Unpublished Ph.D. thesis, University of Aston in Birmingham, 1991), p. 204.

The comparisons between the various parts of Rover closely resemble a study carried out by Pavitt,[15] who analysed 30 industrial sectors to find where and how innovations were generated. The study

INNOVATION ROADBLOCK OR GATEWAY?

identified four clusters, or possible patterns of organisational structure, of the firms:
1. Supplier-dominated firms which rely on external sources.
2. Specialist suppliers of their own design and development.
3. Productive intensive firms, generally driven by a standardisation of processes.
4. Science-based firms, so that innovations can be created through their own research and development activities.

Pavitt's study concluded that 'a high proportion of the knowledge base which underpinned success was actually located inside the firm in forms which were highly tacit and therefore often difficult to transmit to other firms.'[16] This is consistent with Prahalad and Hamel's acclaimed analysis of core competency.[17]

The Rover study found that nearly all innovations were transplants of technology from external suppliers or were techniques generally available in the public domain, and therefore exemplified the simple diffusion processes explored by Rogers.[18] The results of the study show the Rover Group to be an example of Pavitt's supplier-dominated firms. However, there were differences within the Group in the perceptions of innovation: the Land Rover organisation's management and staff wrongly believed that the ideas it had adopted were innovative and unique, whereas the Cowley and Longbridge organisations both rightly perceived that their innovations had been taken from other companies. This is a result of the respective adoption processes: Land Rover's ideas were introduced and developed by engineers and middle managers themselves, whilst the middle management and staff of the car-producing parts of the organisation were not generally involved until new ideas had been decided by senior managers or central group technical staff. It is, as we shall see, a curious fact that Land Rover's mistaken belief in its own innovatory powers is actually a source of strength.

The involvement of the organisation in developing, and so understanding, the innovation or technology appeared to be a key factor in determining how successfully the change was adopted. It also shows that Rover's ability to adopt or learn new technologies, techniques or capabilities may in the future still be deficient, despite the influence of Honda. New ideas have tended to be more successful at Solihull, having been pursued to a conclusion, rather than just petering out as at the volume cars production sites, where many of the ideas have been quickly dropped without being fully implemented. The word adoption should be understood in its fullest sense, that is, treating what is adopted as though it were one's own. This happens at Land Rover, but not at Rover cars, which has been in consequence less successful at incorporating new ideas into the organisation. The laser measuring system at Longbridge, shown in the cover illustration, is a good case. The cell was produced by an outside supplier and during its early life the facility was only switched on for visiting dignitaries, since it produced more data and with greater accuracy than was needed in the manufacturing operation. It took many years to redevelop it into a useable facility, before it was replaced by new, simpler equipment for the R8 replacement in 1995.

Grinyer and Spender, in describing the process of strategy incorporation,[19] use the term 'recipe' to describe an organisation-wide view, either formally or informally maintained, of the organisation's strategies. For a company to progress, they argue, appropriate strategies have to become part of the recipe. In the case of Rover, the data suggest that, for innovations to be successfully adopted, they have to be welcomed by the organisation. Land Rover's ability to ingest ideas and generate the feeling of their belonging to the organisation, irrespective of where they have originated, is well illustrated in the introduction of MRPII, which involved much tailoring of IBM systems to match Land Rover's aspirations. The MRPII ideas were used and enhanced by the Land Rover organisation, and also firmly incorporated into the company's recipes. In the rest of Rover, however, innovations were generally acquired from external sources and superimposed on the organisation by senior management, with no further development or enhancement by the shopfloor management and staff. Ideas have tended to be introduced at Rover Cars by practitioners who are not part of the operational staff, such as Warwick University for the leak testing cell and VETS equipment; Honda for much of the R8 (and the replacement Theta) at Longbridge, the Rover 600 and original Rover 800 manufacturing facilities at Cowley; contracting engineers from equipment suppliers such as Kuka and ASEA for robots; various management consultants for TQI; and ISTEL for many system and communications developments.

Land Rover has a different strategy: the local managers themselves are in charge of the technical decisions and the management of projects. Land Rover may subsequently sub-contract activity to other suppliers like ISTEL and Puma, but only as suppliers and under close supervision. But at Rover cars, much of the organisation is unsympathetic to the process of change. Past failures, as a result of poor understanding at management level, have hampered the development of future projects by eroding the organisation's trust in these external suppliers. Examples are the observed general scepticism concerning Warwick University staff on the part of production managers as a result of developments like the leak testing cell, and more recently the inappropriate and costly introduction of flexible manufacturing systems (FMS) to areas of the firm where the flexibility and added complexity of the systems were not required. This caution will restrict the company's ability to develop new capabilities which are required for it to survive and prosper.

Another aspect of the various innovation processes at Rover is the company's inability to cast off unacceptable or unsuitable technologies and operating paradigms. Organisations which can do this find it easier to be flexible and avoid becoming entrenched in one mode of operation.[20] Land Rover has shown the truth of this by its rejection of unsuitable, previously established production control systems in favour of the MRPII approach. The Rover cars organisations do not have such freedom. Gardiner noted this in his study of Austin Rover's lean[21] designs, which showed Rover unable to discard the hydrogas[22] suspension or transverse engine in favour of more robust alternatives. He concludes that this lost the firm an early advantage it had in the development and manufacture of front-wheel-drive cars.[23] This supports Pavitt's findings that most successful innovation (by which he meant the introduction of something which has a radical effect on the organisation) originates within the organisation. From the Land Rover operating model, a corollary may be inferred, that the innovation can be acquired from outside, provided that the acquisition is welcomed within the firm.

Abernathy's market linkage[24] suggests that Land Rover's innovation capability could be a direct result of its dominant position in a slow-moving market. The company has defended its position through the adoption of a regular incremental approach to improving its products and manufacturing facilities. By being the first into a market of small and limited capacity, Land Rover has previously prevented the competition from gaining a foothold. The small initial size of the market in four-wheel drive, off-road vehicles has, following Land Rover's entry, limited the profit potential for late entries significantly enough to minimise competition for many years. It is only recently that 4x4 leisure vehicles have started to be widely manufactured. Land Rover's response, the Discovery, has held off this competition by utilising existing specialist knowledge and applying it to a new product, much like Cusumano's re-invention, or the adaptation of US technology by the Japanese car industry. Cusumano analysed the absorption of Western ideas into the then struggling embryonic Toyota and Nissan organisations and showed that the organisation's absorption of these ideas was based on a depth of engineering ability, and the re-development of techniques to match the Japanese context.[25] Research has not led to a consensus as to what, with regard to successful innovation, the optimum size of a company might be. Cyert and March suggest that differences of opinion arise from failure to take into account a factor they term relative organisational slack,[26] that is, the freedom from other pressures which allows the organisation, whatever its size, time to innovate. This emphasis on slack, as opposed to size, is consistent with Abernathy's notion of capability linked to the market.[27] Land Rover for many years had no direct competition, and this has allowed it time to develop its products and corresponding innovation methods. By contrast, Rover's car sites have constantly had to operate in a highly competitive market with little or no slack time to innovate or develop a competence in innovation.

This situation can be traced back to the 1920s. At that time, each vehicle was manufactured by skilled people who used their skills to make each part of the product fit correctly, as opposed to mass production, which uses systems for assembling parts which ensure that they should fit together without the need for skilled fitters. Wilkes' imposition of mass production methods on this culture was identified in Whipp and Clark's study of the SD1 project as the main reason for the removal of car manufacturing from the old Rover company's manufacturing plant at Solihull and the failure of BL, in 1981, to make an impression on the saloon car market.[28] The slower moving 4x4 market has proved better suited to Solihull's combination of mass production and craft-based culture. Land Rover has been able to maintain its innovation capability, regarding the crafting of products. It has also used modern methods to ensure the quality and productivity of its manufacturing operations, but this has been severely curtailed by the continued contraction of the firm and the stripping of resources from Solihull for use in other parts of Rover.

These examples of innovation processes within the Rover Group and the differing approaches of the constituent companies bear out what we have said earlier about the K-series engine and 'Rover Tomorrow — The New Deal'. Both these examples of the new Rover's success exemplify the role of Honda in forcing Rover to copy its methods or those of the wider automobile industry. Rover's innovation processes together with its obtaining of design capability from outside — as with the development of models from what are essentially Honda designs — has much in common with what Cusumano observed in the Japanese car industry. But though Rover has had a similar opportunity to acquire Honda's design and manufacturing capabilities, it did not take full advantage. At the time of the company's entry into collaboration with Honda, Rover had the engineering ability to match Cusumano's Toyota and Nissan, but not the capacity for re-invention, which is part of Cusumano's process. That the technology which Rover wished to acquire from Honda was not greatly different from what it already had should have meant that it was easier for Rover to learn. Instead, because it did not have to re-develop the technology, it simply did not trouble to acquire a detailed understanding of it.

Likewise, the lack of ability of Rover cars (as opposed to Land Rover) to introduce new ideas, wherever from, is, for the whole Rover Group, a serious impediment to innovation — or even to profit from the good example shown at Solihull. The capabilities at Land Rover have been heavily diluted. The specialists who were protected under the BL down-sizing have been spread thinly over the rest of the firm, in its efforts to manage the increasing rate of change resulting from the link to Honda and the general direction of the car industry. The collective design capability has been very much reduced from when the relationship with Honda started. The firm is now totally reliant on external sources: suppliers, consultants and BMW. Rover's big successes of recent years have all been based on externally acquired technology: K-series from Honda, Cosworth and other suppliers; Rover Tomorrow from Honda and Nissan; Rover 200, 400, 600 and 800 from Honda. The two successes which have had a large input from Rover itself (1994 Rover 100/Metro and 1994 Range Rover) also owe much to the involvement of suppliers and the now widely practised tools of simultaneous engineering and parts carry-over. Perhaps more telling is the need for Rover to deploy nearly all its available engineering resources on two projects which were in effect developments of existing models, engines and production facilities. The Rover 100 was a development of an existing model, extending the use of the K-series engine and Peugeot-derived R65 gearbox, whilst the Range Rover replacement programme was started in 1988 and took seven years to enter production. Presently, Land Rover is able to manage the timely renewal of its products, but only, as we have seen, because the market it dominates is by its very nature slow-moving. The car manufacturing side seems lost without Honda. Following the sale by BAe of Rover to BMW, Honda's long-term role looks to have ended. Can BMW fill the vacuum left, or will Rover be expected to concentrate on the small, medium and four-wheel drive market sectors, which are missing from the parent company's portfolio?

These are questions which can only be answered by BMW's senior management, but it is clear that innovation and product renewal do not just appear out of thin air. They require substantial financial resources and costly labour time. BMW was and always will be a relatively strong player in Europe with a product range which sells at premium prices. Whether BMW can turn Rover into the same premium priced front-wheel-drive based product range is another matter. To take the Rover business into this territory would drain precious cash resources from BMW and affect the company's ability to maintain development of the 3, 5 and 7 series. Nor is it yet clear whether Rover can stand alone as a separate financial division, and here the picture is much less certain. As long as Land Rover continues to do well, it will generate enough cash at least for the funding of incremental new process and product innovations.

Notes

1. J.B. Quinn, 'Managing Innovation: Controlled Chaos', *Innovation: Harvard Business Review Collection* (Cambridge, MA, 1991), p. 17.
2. C. Freeman, *The Economics of Industrial Innovation* (Cambridge, MA, 1982), p. 112.
3. J.A. Schumpeter, *Business Cycles* (New York, 1939); J. Jewkes, D. Sawers and R. Stillerman, *The Sources of Invention* (London, 1958).
4. J.G. March and H.A. Simon, *Organisations* (New York, 1958); J. Woodward, *Industrial Organisations Theory and Practice* (Oxford, 1980); T. Burns and G.M. Stalker, *The Management of Innovation* (London, 1961).
5. R. Whipp and P.A. Clark, *Innovation in the Auto Industry* (London, 1986), p. 7.
6. R. Roy and D. Wield (eds.), *Product Design and Technological Innovation* (Milton Keynes, 1989).
7. E.M. Rogers, *Diffusion of Innovation* (New York, 1962); also see Freeman, *Economics of Industrial Innovation*, Ch. 5.
8. Rogers, *Diffusion*.
9. Ibid.; N. Gross, J. Giacquinta and M. Bernstein, *Implementing Organizational Innovations* (New York, 1971); also see the discussion in P.A. Clark, *Anglo-American Innovation* (Berlin, 1987), Ch. 3.
10. W.J. Abernathy, *Productivity Dilemma* (London, 1978); M.A. Cusumano, 'Manufacturing Innovation: Lessons from the Japanese Auto Industry', *Sloan Management Review* (Fall, 1988), p. 29.
11. P.A. Clark and N. Staunton, *Innovation in Technology and Organisation* (London, 1989), p. 61.
12. J. Utterbeck and W.J. Abernathy, 'A Dynamic Model of Process and Product Innovation', *Omega*, Vol. 3 No. 6 (1975), pp. 639-56.
13. A. Pilkington, 'Japanese Production Strategies and Competitive Success: Mazda's Quiet Revolution', *Journal of Far Eastern Business*, Vol. 1 No. 4 (1995), pp. 15-35.
14. For more information see A. Pilkington, 'A Study of Strategy Formulation in an Automotive Manufacturer' (Unpublished Ph.D. thesis, University of Aston in Birmingham, 1991), Appendix B.
15. K. Pavitt, 'Sectoral Patterns of Technical Change', *Research Policy*, Vol. 13 (1984), pp. 343-73.
16. Clark and Staunton, *Innovation*, p. 174.
17. C.K. Prahalad and G. Hamel, 'The Core Competence of the Corporation', *Harvard Business Review* (May-June 1990), pp. 79-91.
18. Rogers, *Diffusion*.
19. P. Grinyer and J. Spender, *Turnaround: Managerial Recipes for Strategic Success* (London, 1979).
20. Clark and Staunton, *Innovation*, p. 13.
21. Gardiner denotes lean designs as those which limit the future ability to be adapted into new and still competitive products. Robust designs can be extended into new models for little or no additional design cost.
22. A suspension system which links the different axles, not through the standard mechanical system, but using hydraulics, and is still in use by Rover in the MGF.

23. J.P. Gardiner, 'Robust and Lean Designs with State of the Art Automotive and Aircraft Examples', in C. Freeman (ed.), *Design Innovation and Long Cycles in Economic Development* (London, 1986), Ch. 8.
24. W.J. Abernathy, K. Clark and A. Kantrow, *Industrial Renaissance*, p. 28.
25. M.A. Cusumano, *The Japanese Automobile Industry* (Cambridge, MA, 1985).
26. R.M. Cyert and J.G. March, *A Behavioural Theory of the Firm* (Englewood Cliffs, NJ, 1963), pp. 278-9.
27. Abernathy, *Productivity Dilemma*.
28. Whipp and Clark, *Innovation in the Auto Industry*.

8

Restructuring the European Car Industry: Lessons from Rover

The end of British-owned volume car production
Financial Times, 1 February 1994

In this final chapter we raise a number of questions which pertain to the European motor industry. How much can Rover tell us about the future development of the European car industry? To answer this we will consider three aspects of the Rover experience which have something in common with emerging and more general conditions faced by European manufacturers. First, Rover illustrates how changing market fortunes can undermine the financial performance of a business. What lessons can we draw from this for the future European car market? Secondly, at each stage of the experience plans and policies designed to reduce costs and improve resource efficiency came to nought, because they failed to transform the fundamental financial situation of the business. Again, what general lessons might European car manufacturers learn? Finally, after the Honda relationship ended BMW claimed what was left of a hollowed-out business. What conclusions can be drawn about weak European companies which become dependent on others for product and process innovation? In the end, weak companies are often taken over and restructured, and within the politics of European integration this makes sense in so far as rationalisation delivers economies of scale.

The problems of market saturation forced the amalgamation of UK car manufacturers into BL. There was no longer sufficient expansion in sales to support the number of firms in the market. The smaller firms were weak in comparison with their competitors, and became the subject of takeovers. The same forces which dogged the independents, and led to the super-conglomerate BL, continued to threaten the prospects and financial performance of the new firm. This led to the cancellation of new model projects, further damaging the image of the firm, its standing in the market, its sales, and the prospects of future capital funding. Yet at this time the firm did have several strengths, such as a large share of the market, strong exports, design capability and Land Rover. The Ryder rescue plan of 1975 continued the approach which had seen the majority of the UK motor manufacturers join together, a strategy of increasing production to secure economies of scale. Unfortunately, in the stagnant UK market of the late 1970s, overproduction was the wrong strategy to select. Financial troubles mounted, despite large and frequent injections of public money. Edwardes brought a different approach to bear by concentrating on the production of a limited number of models and reducing sales targets. The lost share of the UK market was irrecoverably taken up, both by long standing competitors, and by new entrants to the market from mainland Europe and Japan. Edwardes tried to revitalise the firm's product range and manufacturing processes through forming a relationship with Honda. Unfortunately, the plans of the rationalised firm relied on funds generated through increased sales which did not materialise. The firm was further hit by the slump in the market and its financial position weakened further. Rover never recovered the volumes lost during 1976-80, as poor industrial relations drained the funds set aside for projects necessary to maintain existing levels of sales.

There is an important lesson for the future of the European car industry, which is itself now nearing the levels of saturation first seen in the UK during the late 1970s. Table 8.1 suggests that new car ownership in Europe is reaching a natural limit of one for each economically active individual. This is very likely one of the causes of the ending of large cyclical variations between boom and lean years, as shown in Table 8.2. The *Economist* Intelligence Unit maintains that the potential for Europe's new car market to return to the pre-recession level of around 13.5 million *per annum*, achieved in 1991-92, is limited. 'After recovering to 13.15 million in 1996 new car sales are forecast by the EIU to remain within the range 13-13.5 million for the rest of the decade.'[1] The same pressures which came to bear on BL in the 1980s, and forced it into rationalisation and losses in its market share, are developing in the rest of Europe. The new competition in the UK market of the 1980s came from continental Europe and Japan. Japanese firms used low prices to generate an opening in the then highly profitable UK market. These new entrants picked up the sales Rover had lost, whilst the other two large UK producers, Ford and Vauxhall, maintained or increased their market shares by importing vehicles from mainland Europe (see Table 1.5), and by taking action to improve productivity. New market entrants in the European market during the 1990s are the Japanese transplant operations, which have added an extra production capacity within Europe of around 1.2 million cars.[2] There is also fierce competition from the newly industrialised countries (NICs), such as Korea and Malaysia. The NICs are able to pay lower wages to keep costs and prices low. They offer attractive specifications and are capturing a growing share of the European market, in much the same way as Japanese firms did in the 1980s in Britain.

Table 8.1
Cars in Use (Not New Sales) and Levels of Ownership in Europe, 1967-91

	Cars in Use in the Twelve EU Countries	Cars per Economically Active Person
1967	45,952,454	0.37
1975	77,007,125	0.65
1987	116,004,474	0.67
1991	134,790,178	0.94

Source: C. Haslam and S. Johal, 'Cyclical Recovery and Structural Problems: European Cars in the 1990s', *Engineering Management Journal,* Vol. 5 No. 5 (Oct. 1995), pp. 201-5.

At Rover, Day continued the policy of rationalisation begun by Edwardes. He also introduced tight cost controls whilst simultaneously trying to move the products up-market. The strategy was designed to attract customers willing to pay premium prices for cars which bore the newly relaunched Rover 'viking ship' badge. The new products offered greater luxury and performance compared to the standard models offered by competitors. It was supposed that the volume of sales available would ensure that the company's costs were recovered. However, this strategy faltered with the onset of world recession. Rover was forced to cut margins further in the UK. The company had become dependent on the UK market, because the infrastructure needed to compete in Europe had long since been dismantled. Not only was Rover forced to sell at minimum profit; it was also selling fewer cars.

Table 8.2
The Cycles of European Car Sales, 1973-91

Years	Per Cent Fall between Peak and Trough Years
1973-74	-12.7
1979-81	-7.5
1990-91	-4.7

Source: Various *SMMT Year Books*.

In the late 1980s and early 1990s Rover introduced further cost control methods, in order to boost productivity. Japanese product and process innovations were introduced with the help of Honda, as were changes in the pay structures and methods such as Total Quality and benchmarking. Rover committed itself to reducing costs in line with those of its competitors. As already discussed, a near three-fold improvement was achieved in the 20 years to 1990 (Table 3.8), in line with the gains seen elsewhere in Europe (Table 8.3). This, however, failed to restore Rover to a strong financial position. The profits which were reported from 1988 were later wiped out by subsequent losses. The continued financial restructuring of the company through the transfer of assets to BAe and other firms did not change this position (Table 1.6). The same pattern can be seen in the European car industry, as other major manufacturers have undertaken similar types of cost reduction and efficiency improvements (Table 8.3). There has been negligible improvement in subsequent financial results. Firms such as VW and Peugeot-Citroen have struggled into profitability during 1994, whilst others are still returning losses. Restructuring and cost reduction strategies across Europe have been preceded by moves similar to those that Rover made into quality management, such as Ford's much publicised campaigns of the late 1980s. Car manufacturers have tried different strategies to reduce costs: VW moved to acquire Seat and Skoda, Fiat and Renault experimented with automation and robotics, and others, for example Peugeot, have negotiated new working agreements with employees.

Table 8.3
Crude Cars per Employee per Year for Various Countries, 1979-89

	France	Germany	Italy	Spain	UK
1979	7.3	5.9	5.5	n/a	3.1
1980	n/a	n/a	n/a	7.4	n/a
1981	6.6	5.4	5.3	6.8	3.3
1982	7.2	5.6	5.5	8.9	3.7
1983	7.6	5.7	6.5	9.2	4.4
1984	7.3	5.5	7.1	9.5	4.0
1985	7.7	5.9	7.5	10.5	4.9
1986	8.7	5.9	9.1	11.5	4.9
1987	9.8	5.9	9.6	12.3	5.5
1988	10.5	5.9	10.4	13.5	6.0
1989	11.4	6.2	10.7	14.3	6.3

Source: K. Williams, C. Haslam, S. Johal and J. Williams, *Cars: Analysis, History, Cases,* (Oxford, 1994).

Rover's relationship with Honda was characterised by growing dependency and a weakening financial structure. By 1993, less than one-third of Rover's production consisted of its own models, compared with 95 per cent in 1981. This raised the fear that Rover would become an off-shore manufacturing plant, just as Edwardes had warned it might when Renault was considered as a partner for a joint venture in 1980.[3] What did Rover learn from its collaboration with Honda? The company certainly gained in design capability: ageing vehicles were replaced with modern, desirable products that were often described as leaders in the field by the motoring press. But whether the company would be able to absorb this capability was soon open to question. Rover was able to produce its new range in collaboration with Honda. It remained, however, financially vulnerable. Would the company be able to maintain the same level of design competency in its new relationship with BMW? Through Honda, Rover acquired an insight into world-class manufacturing techniques and technology. The facilities at Oxford and Birmingham were able to produce cars at quality levels unheard of in the days of BL and at productivity levels close to those of their European competitors. Moreover, Japanese management techniques were introduced, leading, among other things, to the creation of single status canteens and company uniforms. New pay structures were introduced to shift responsibility for production performance away from desk-bound management to the shopfloor workers.[4]

The problematic nature of the relationship between Honda and the BMW-owned Rover may have been foreseen by the executives in Munich, but it cannot assist future development at Cowley or Longbridge, now that the Honda-Rover relationship appears to have little or no future. The rear-wheel-drive design capability at BMW differs from that of front-wheel-drive Honda, which has left its legacy at Rover. Can the British company evolve capabilities independently of Honda, whilst providing BMW with the insight it seeks into Japanese working methods? Additionally, BMW may have sought entry into the rapidly expanding 4x4 market, as well as increasing its control of executive car sales.

An important lesson of the Rover and Honda collaboration — evident after a decade or so — is that strategic intentions should not have been forgotten; a policy of 'pragmatic' adjustments led gradually to a weakened design capability and loss of independence. Unlike Rover, Honda pursued its long-term goals. It is fair to note that the Rover-Honda relationship was not typical of collabora-

Plate 8.1 John Towers and Bernd Pischetsrieder with an MGRV8 at Gaydon, 1994

tive ventures in the car industry from the 1980s, because of the British company's desperate plight. But the international management literature is only just beginning to reflect the broad compass of joint venture strategies. These are evident in the growing number of collaborative projects in the world car industry. NUMMI (New United Motor Manufacturing Inc.), for example, allows Toyota to build cars in the US and General Motors the opportunity to learn Japanese methods at first hand. Collaboration has moved beyond the goals of market entry and the spreading of risks, towards that of the joint acquisition of design and manufacturing capabilities. What is also clear from the story of Rover and Honda is that Rover's initial sense of crisis stemmed in part from its history, as well as the disparate aims and cultures of its antecedent firms. The potential benefits of collaboration were, however, dissipated by continued tensions over product and production strategies. This often happens in a relationship between a weak partner and a strong one. The weaker partner may achieve the desired transformation if the stronger partner continues to control or withhold its particular competitive advantage. Current thinking on international joint ventures concerns itself largely with the *external* dimensions of the firm — questions of market entry and commercial risk bearing — but in matters of capability exchange and organisational learning it is the *internal* institutional settings and their historical roots which need to be understood.

The sale of Rover to BAe raised hopes that the former could continue as an independent car manufacturer. Unfortunately, Rover's fate had already been sealed by factors beyond its control. BAe's financial position was not strong enough to allow it to continue its support, in the face of Rover's weakening position in markets which were being shaped by cost-cutting competitors in a declining market. BAe's own financial crisis led it to pass Rover to the cash-rich BMW (see Plate 8.1). This takeover has confirmed the ending of a British owned, volume car manufacturer, though it does not mark the end of the Rover story.

Analysts have discussed at some length the reasons why BMW paid £800m for Rover. Most agree that the need to gain an insight into Japanese production methods and the opportunity to acquire a manufacturer at a knock-down price were the main reasons. Two other reasons also seem significant: first, the market position of Land

Rover, and second, the relatively low levels of costs in British manufacturing industry compared to Germany. Other countries with low wage costs such as Spain and Portugal do not possess Northern European levels of infrastructure, transport facilities, and a traditional car industry. The policies of the present British government will let this situation continue for as long as it remains in office, and it is unlikely that a change of government will do much to reverse the trend. The clusters of suppliers forming around the Japanese transplant operations in the UK will mean a plentiful supply of cheap, high-quality parts, such as is not available elsewhere in Europe. Rover also fits in well with BMW's market structures. BMW has a high reputation for expensive, rear-wheel-drive vehicles. In contrast, Rover has a growing reputation for quality front-wheel-drive cars as well as four-wheel-drives. It has a strong presence in the UK, one of Europe's bigger markets. BMW's strategy for Rover is only known by a few executives in Munich, but in any case Rover is no longer a force in the world car industry. Market share, production capacity and sales have fallen to about half 1973 levels; the resources of the firm and its capabilities have been effectively stripped away to create a leaner, fitter organisation.

Rover's progression along a route of failure, restructuring and merger, is one that ultimately led to its takeover. Financial constraints created by market conditions mean that the smaller and weaker European car manufacturers will be unable to sustain their new product renewal and innovative activities. These firms will be forced to share their research and development activities with bigger competitors. The Rover-Honda partnership illustrates the point. In an overcrowded car market, there will be further takeovers. Evidence for this trend is already available in the shape of several smaller European manufacturers like Seat, and Jaguar; and parts of the Swedish car industry. The Swedish case has many parallels with Rover; Saab was bought by GM, and Volvo attempted to develop a partnership with the much larger Renault. Volvo, like Rover in 1990, is too small to fund its model renewal activity. It has undergone some restructuring, including transferring operations to the Netherlands, ironically after incorporating the failing DAF manufacturer. It has now been forced to enter a joint venture with Renault in order to cut costs. Volvo has clung to a strategy based on selling solid and safe products in contrast to Rover's policy of product differentiation.

The prospect is for a predatory restructuring of the European car industry which will see an increasing concentration of market share and further honing of costs. Duplicate activities will be cancelled as production and support activities are transferred in order to make better use of existing capacity. Competition from new entrants like Hyundai, Daewoo and Proton will lead to high-specification vehicles at prices which will undercut European products because of advantages in labour costs. European car makers will have to rethink their sourcing strategies, and consider finding cheaper parts supplies in countries like Korea, China and Mexico. Large automotive component firms like Bosch and Lucas are already developing overseas operations and joint ventures.

If events in continental Europe continue to replicate the past experiences of the UK, Rover's story will be re-enacted in the future. Concentration will increase as car firms amalgamate. This will be politically acceptable on the grounds that rationalisation should deliver economies of scale, continued employment, and maintain trade levels, as was argued when BL was nationalised. Eventually, only a few European manufacturers will be left. This may, however, be a prolonged process. After all, it took Rover 30 years to reach its present position. Eventually, however, Rover had little say as its future was overtaken by changing market conditions and shifts in the wider global economy − a renewal of sorts?

Notes

1. *Financial Times*, 12 July 1994.
2. J. Womack, D. Jones and D. Roos, *The Machine That Changed the World* (London, 1990), p. 203.
3. M. Edwardes, *Back from the Brink* (London, 1983), p. 194.
4. J. Towers, 'A New Deal?', *Manufacturing Engineer* (July 1992), pp. 45-7.

Index

A-Series engine, 133-4
Abernathy, William, 24, 34, 40, 151, 157
Acclaim, Triumph, 14, 73-5
Accord, Honda, 18, 76-8
Advanced Technology Centre, Warwick University, 101-9
Aerostructures Hamble, 112
Aircraft manufacturing, 8
Allegro, Austin, 14
Aluminimum engines, 132, 135
Alvis, 9, 11
Advanced Manufacturing Technology (AMT), 95, 111
AMT, *see* Advanced Manufacturing Technology
Arthur Anderson, 124
Aston, University of, xi, 109
Aston Martin, 64
AT&T, 142
Austin, Herbert, 7, 9, 10, 13, 17-19, 66
Austin Allegro, 14
Austin Metro, *see* Metro
Austin Maxi, *see* Maxi
Austin Princess, 14
Automobile Association, 9

Baden-Fuller, Charles, 116, 125-6

BAe, 18, 19, 78, 82, 104, 112, 120, 126, 143, 160, 166, 170
BAe, Aerostructures Hamble, 112
Ballade, Honda, 14, 75-8
Barr, Andy, 101-3
Benchmarking, 124-5, 166
Bertodo, Roland, 120
Bhattacharyya, Kumar, 101-3
Birmingham University, 98, 102
Birmingham Polytechnic, 95
BL, 3, 7, 9-10, 12, 14, 17, 19, 38, 58, 60, 62, 72, 102, 122, 131, 158
BL, restructuring, 9-18, 163-4
BL Systems Ltd, *see* ISTEL
BMW, ix, xi, 1, 6, 21, 60, 63, 83-4, 138, 145, 160, 163, 168
BMW, design expertise, 149, 168
Body-in-white, 27
Bosch, 172
BP, 118, 123-4
Breakthrough, 18, 116-128
British Aerospace, *see* BAe
British Government, *see* Government, UK
British Leyland, *see* BL
British Motor Heritage Trust, xii

British Petroleum, *see* BP
Burns, Tom, 149

Capability, 4, 6, 19, 87, 90, 127, 148-9, 159, 168, 171
Capability acquisition, x
Capability, innovation, 151
Capability in Rover, 120, 164
Capability, Land Rover, 158
Capacity, production, *see* Overcapacity
Carry-over, design, 40-43, 136
Cell management at Rover, 106
Cell, U-shaped, 48
Chandler, Alfred, 3
China, 172
Chrysler, 26, 60, 73
Church, Roy, 10
Citroen, 26, 60, 166
Civic, Honda, 67, 76-8, 132
Clark, Kim, 40
Clark, Peter, xi, 8, 158
Collaboration, *see* International Joint Venture (IJV)
Competition, 172
Competition, influence on innovation, 158
Competition, UK market, 164
Complexity, 43, 143
Concerto, Honda, 76, 136
Concurrent engineering, *see* Simultaneous engineering
Conway, Bill, 124
Core competence, 62, *also see* Prahalad, C.K.
Cosby, Phil, 116
Cosworth Engineering, 136
Coventry City Council, 110
Cowley, 7, 10, 13, 16-19, 81, 151
Cowley, production control system, 143
Craft-based production, 8, 17, 158
Curtis, Alan, 112
Cusumano, Michael, 25, 43, 151, 158
Cycle manufacturing, 7, 66

Daewoo, 60, 172
DAF, 171
Daihatsu, 61, 64
Day, Graham, 7, 17, 19, 120, 165
Defender, Land Rover, 143
Delco, 49
Demming, W.E., 44, 116
Department of Trade and Industry, 97
Design, 59-61
Design lead times, 41, 138
Design for manufacture, 40
Design process, 39-44, 133
Discovery, Land Rover, 126, 158
Dolomite, Triumph, 14
Drucker, Peter, 116

Economy, global, 65
Economy, UK, 10
Edwardes, Michael, 12, 14, 25, 35, 58, 72-5, 139, 164, 168
Efficiency, 25, 35, 84
Engines, x, 75-6, 82, 131-7, 152
Engines, used in Rover collaborations, 75
European car industry, 163-72
European car market, 164

European Union, 20, 62
Expansion, 12

Fiat, 26, 60, 63-4, 167
Financial performance at BL-Rover, 128, 160, 163-4, 166
First World War, 7
Flow layout, 46, 48
Flexible Manufacturing System (FMS), 104, 152, 157
FMS, see Flexible Manufacturing System
Ford UK, 10, 43, 60, 64, 165
Ford, After Japan Programme, 55
Ford, Highland Park, 24
Ford, Model T, 10, 43
Ford, Sierra, 40
Freeman, Christopher, 149-50
Freight Rover, 17, 102
Friesen, Peter, 3-4, 119
Fujimoto, Takahiro, 40
Fujisawa, Takeo, 67

Gardiner, J.P., 41, 136
Gas Turbine, 8-9
General Motors, see GM
General Motors Institute, 94, 101
Globalisation, 62, 64-5, 151, 163-72
GM, 26, 36, 55, 61, 64, 73, 171
GM, NUMMI, see NUMMI
Goldratt, Eli, 116
Government, UK, 3, 12, 20, 171

Hamel, Garry, 4, 122, 155
Harrison, Alan, 44
Honda, x, 1, 7, 18, 25, 39, 58-87, 90, 115, 127, 145-6, 163-4, 168
Honda Accord, 18, 76-8
Honda Ballade, 14, 75-8
Honda Civic, 67, 76-8, 132
Honda Concerto, 76, 136
Honda, design skills, 159
Honda, influence on Land Rover, 155
Honda, influence on Rover capability, 74, 80, 85, 106, 132, 159-60
Honda Legend, 43
Honda, manufacturing strategy, 71, 123, 142
Honda, motorcycles, 67
Honda, Soichiro, 66-9
Horton, Bill, 102
Hunt, Gilbert, 110
Hyundai, 26, 61, 172

IBM, 144, 156
IJV, see International Joint Venture
Imperial Rover Motor Cycle, 7
IMVP, 1, 25, 28, 39, 124
Infinity, Nissan, 76
Innovation, xi, 24, 34, 39, 127, 148-160, 163
Innovation, adoption by adaptation, 156, 159-60
Innovation, contingency specific, 152
Innovation in the Japanese car industry, 151
Innovation, orthodox theory, 149
Institute of Mechanical Engineers, 93

Integrated Graduate Development Scheme (IGDS), 104
International Joint Venture (IJV), 58-87, 90, 163, 170
Ishikakwa or Fishbone Diagram, 45-6
ISTEL, 19, 126, 142, 144, 156-7
Isuzu, 60
Ital, Morris, 14

Jaguar, 14, 17, 60, 64
Japanese management, 168
Japanese management in Rover, *see* Rover Tomorrow
Japanese manufacturing, *see* Lean production
Japanese universities, 94
Jewkes, J, 149
JIT, *see* Just-in-Time
Jones, Dan, 124
Juran, J.M., 116
Just-in-Time, *see* Lean production

K-Series engine, x, 76, 82, 131-7, 152
Kaizen, 46, 118
Kanban, 49, 142, *also see* Lean production
Kanter, R.M., 116
Kay, John, 6, 18, 117
Kayser, Frank, 9
KIA, 60
Korea, 165, 172

Lanchester (Coventry) Polytechnic, 110
Lancia, 63

Land Rover, 8, 17-19, 170-1
Land Rover Defender, 143
Land Rover, design capability, 158
Land Rover Discovery, 126, 158
Land Rover, innovation, 148, 152-60
Land Rover, MRPII Systems, 142-5, 152
Land Rover Parts Ltd, 20, 139
Land Rover, Range Rover, 8, 14, 160
Land Rover, technical capability, 157
Le Mans 24-Hour Race, 9
Lean production, 1, 24-5, 34-55, 142-4, 168, 170
Lean production at Rover, 34-5, 106, 124-6
Legend, Honda, 43
Lewis, Edmund, 7
Lexus, Toyota, 76
Leyland, 9, 12, *also see* BL
Life cycles, 151
LM10/11 Programme, *see* Maestro *or* Montego
Loctite, 136
Longbridge, 7, 9, 17-19, 75, 132, 151
Longbridge, production control system, 143
Lotus, 64
Low Pressure Sand Casting Process, 136
Lucas, 49, 104, 172
Lucas-Birmingham University relationship, 109-10
Lyons, William, 110

Maestro, Austin, 18, 133
Maintenance, TPM, 48-9
Mair, Andrew, 66, 69
Malaysia, 165
Manufacturing Resource Planning, *see* MRPII
Manufacturing strategy at Rover, 108, 125
March, J.G., 149
Marina, Morris, 14
Market conditions, 128
Market entry, 157, 168, 170
Market, European, 164-5
Market share, Rover, 15, 20, 138, 164-6, 171
Market, UK, 19-20, 121, 131, 148, 163-5
Mass production, 8, 10, 18, 158
Mather, Hal, 117, 124
Maudsley, 8
Maxi, Austin, 14
Mazda, 25, 35, 60, 64, 151
Mazda, MX5, 39
Mercedes Benz, 8, 55
Metro, 14, 18, 79, 82, 160
Metro, engine, 132-3
Mexico, 172
MG, 14, 18, 79, 160
MGRV8, 169
MIC, JIT at Rover, 142-3, 152
Miller, Danny, 3-4, 119
Mini, 14, 79, 82, 133
Minimal Inventory Control, *see* MIC
Mintzberg, Henry, 3-4, 6, 117, 119
MITI, 67
Mitsubishi, 26, 60
Mixed-model production, 39

Model T Ford, 10, 43
Monden, Y, 25
Montego, Austin, 18, 133
Morris, William, Lord Nuffield, 7, 10, 13, 16, 17-19, 34
Morris, Marina, 14
Morris, Ital, 14
Motorcycles, Honda, 67
MRPII, 142-5, 156
MX5, Mazda, 39

Nationalisation, 3
New Deal, the, *see* Rover Tomorrow
New model programmes, 171
New product development at Rover, 160, 163-4
New United Motor Manufacturing Inc., *see* NUMMI
Nissan, 8, 25, 60, 64
Nissan, Infinity, 76
Nissan Sunny, 132
Nissan, Washington, 122
NUMMI, 55, 64, 170

O-Series engine, 133
OECD, 91
Ohno, Taichi, 25, 117
Organisation structure and change, ix, 3, 116, 119
Organisational renewal, 1, 24, 26, 55, 65, 73, 115-27, 167, 171-2
Over-capacity, Europe, 164-5
Over-capacity, Rover, 13, 70
Over-capacity, United States, 65

P-Series of Rover cars, 9, 17
Parallel engineering, *see*

Simultaneous engineering
Parnaby, John, 110
Pascale, Richard Tanner, 69, 117, 119-20
Pavitt, K., 154-5
Peters, Tom, 117
Peugeot, 26, 55, 60, 166
Peugeot and Rover collaboration, *see* R65
Ph.D., industry-based, 97, 105
Philips Electrical, 101
Pischetrieder, Bernd, 169
Poka-yoke, 45
Porsche, 26
Porter, Michael, 2, 59, 117
Prahalad, C.K., 4, 122, 155
Pressed Steel, 7, 10
Princess, Austin, 14
Product differentiation, 171-2
Product differentiation, Rover, 7-8, 17, 81, 165-6, 171
Product life cycle, 151
Production volume, 2, 13, 164, 166
Productivity, 17, 85, 164, 166-7
Profits, 9, 19, 72, 128, 131, 139, 148, 166
Profits at Rover, 19, 128, 139
Pull manufacturing control, *see* Lean production
Push manufacturing control, *see* MRPII

QS2000, 6
Quinn, James Brian, 3, 148

R65 gearbox, 79, 132, 138, 160
R8, 18, 35, 75-8, 82, 104, 132, 156

Range Rover, 8, 14, 160
Rejuvenation theory, 116
Renewal, 1, 24, 26, 55, 65, 73, 115-27, 167, 171-2
Restructuring, 166
Restructuring, BL-Rover, 9-18, 159, 163-4, 171
Restructuring, European car industry, ix, xi, 2, 163-72
Robust design, 41, 136
Rogers, E.M., 149-150, 155
Rolls Royce aero engines, 107
Rolls Royce cars, 65
Rootes, Lord, 110
Rover Assisted Learning Scheme, 105
Rover 100, *see* Metro
Rover 200/400, 1990-1995, *see* R8
Rover 200/400 1995 model, *see* Theta
Rover 200, 1984-1990, Project XX, 75
Rover 600, 18, 76-8, 82, 156
Rover 800, 18, 43, 75-6, 82, 126, 156
Rover Learning Business, 105
Rover Safety Cycle, 7
Rover SD1, 12, 14, 158
Rover Tomorrow, 131, 139-42, 145, 152, 168
Ryder, Don, 10, 12, 122, 164

S-Series engine, 133
Saab, 26, 60, 63-4, 171
Sakiya, T., 69-70
Sales, 171, *also see* Markets
Schaffer, R., 118-9
Schonberger, Richard, 117

Schumpeter, J., 149
Science and Engineering Research Council, 97-8
Science parks, 98-9
Seat, 167
Second World War, 8
Seneffe, Belgium, 13
Set-up time, 46
Shingo, Shigeo, 47, 117
Shopfloor management, 168
Shopfloor management at Rover, *see* Rover Tomorrow
Sierra, Ford, 40
Simon, H.A., 149
Simpson, George, 18, 117, 120, 122-3
Simultaneous engineering, 40, 133
Skoda, 26, 167
Smith, Charles, & Associates, 19, 123
Solihull, 13, 17, 151-2
SPC, 45
Speke, 13
Spitfire, Triumph, 14
Stag, Triumph, 14
Stagnation of European and UK markets, 163-5
Stalker, G.M., 149
Starley, John, 7, 66
Sterling Motor Company, 76, 127, *also see* Rover 800
Statistical Process Control, *see* SPC
Stock levels at Rover, 106
Stopford, John, 116, 125-6
Strachan, Ian, xii
Strategy, 62, 156, 168
Strategic advantage, 2, 6

Strategic aspirations of Rover, 120-1
Strategy at Rover, 149
Subaru, 60
Supercub, Honda, 67
Suppliers, 6, 27, 45
Suppliers, as an innovation source, 155
Suppliers, in a JIT system, 49-55
Suppliers, involvement in design, 133-5
Sutton, William, 7
Suzuki, 26, 60, 132
Sweden, 171
Swindon, 63, 78

Takeover, 9, 171
Teaching company, 97-8
Technology life cycle, 151
Theta, 18, 156
Towers, John, 131, 169
Toyota, 25, 34, 60
Toyota, Burnaston, 122
Toyota, Lexus, 76
Toyota, NUMMI, 64, 170
Toyota, problem solving, 46
Toyota, strategy, 151
Toyota production system, *see* Lean production
Total Quality Management, *see* TQM
TPM, 48-9
TQM, 24, 44-6, 166
TQM at Rover, TQI, 140, 153, 156
TR7, Triumph, 14
Trade unions, 14, 132, 139, 164
Transformational Technology

Inc., 118
Transnational corporations, 2
Transplant operations, 71-73, 82-3, 149, 168, 171
Triumph, 13, 14
Triumph, Dolomite, 14
Triumph TR7, 14
Tyseley, 8

U-shaped cell, 48
UK car market, 19-20, 121, 131, 148, 163-5
Unipart, 139
University-industry consortia, 96-7, 100-1
University-industry relations, 90-112
US Clean Air Act, 67

V-TEC Engine, Honda, 84, 138
Vauxhall, 10, 36, 165
Vertical integration, 125
Volkswagon, *see* VW
Volume of car production, 2, 13, 164, 166
Volvo, 26, 40, 61, 171
VW, 26, 60, 64, 166

Warwick University, x, 90-112, 156
Warwickshire County Council, 110
Whipp, Richard, 8, 158
Wight, Olie, 117
Wilks, S.B., 8, 17
Williams, K., *et al.*, 25, 131
Wolfson Foundation, 100
Wolseley, 9, 18
Womack, J., *et al.*, 1, 25, 28,

39, 124
Woodward, Joan, 149